FRIENDLY FOOD

Rosemary Stanton

Photography
Ray Joyce

Illustrations
Barbara Rodanska

MURDOCH BOOKS
Sydney • London

THE HEALTHY WAY

Welcome to the delights of healthy eating! Some people worry that healthy foods may lack flavour. Let me assure you that the recipes in this book are not only good for you, they also taste delicious. Wherever possible, they are low in fat, salt and sugar and high in dietary fibre. Many are also great sources of calcium and other nutrients to keep your body vitally healthy.

There is no doubt that we need to make some changes to the typical Western diet. Many health problems are related to what we eat and the greatest dietary culprit is fat. An excess of salt and sugar and a lack of dietary fibre are also problems. If we want healthier foods, we have no option but to go back to the kitchen. This is not a sentence, but a pleasure – especially if tasks are shared.

Healthy eating means giving more attention to the wonderful range of foods available. Luscious fruits, fresh vegetables, pasta, rice and other grains, the marvellous variety of breads, succulent seafoods, tender cuts of chicken and the leanest of meats have so much to offer – in taste and in health benefits. Spices and herbs can give flavour in a much more interesting way than salt.

My philosophy about eating is to be healthy, not fanatical. The quantities of fat and sugar have been kept to the minimum consistent with great flavour. None of the recipes has added salt but there are always flavoursome ingredients.

But I must warn you. After cooking the healthy way, you'll find it impossible to return to greasy or fatty foods, or to meals whose major flavour is that of salt. Healthy eating seduces your taste-buds so that they crave good foods.

There are a few facts you should know about the recipes. The fat content of each recipe is listed. For weight loss, keep fat to 30-40 grams a day. If you work hard physically or play a lot of strenuous sport, aim for a maximum of 55-65 grams. For others, a daily total of 45-60 grams will decrease the risk of many common health problems. The kind of fat is also important, especially to reduce risks of heart disease and cancer. Olive oil is the best choice.

Average daily sodium requirements range from 920-2300 mg. All recipes listed as being low sodium have less than 120 mg sodium per serve.

A desirable daily intake of dietary fibre is 30-40 grams. In recipes described as excellent, an average serve will have more than 7.5 g of fibre. A 'very good' fibre content is 5 g and a 'good' rating is 3 g.

Where small amounts of sugar or honey have been used, the recipe contains some dietary fibre to slow down the rate at which sugar enters the blood.

Recipes described as rich in calcium have as much calcium as you would find in a glass of milk. Recipes which provide more than 70 per cent of the recommended daily intake (RDI) of a vitamin or mineral are described as 'excellent'; 'very good' sources provide 50 per cent; a 'good' source has at least 25 per cent; 'useful' sources have more than 15 per cent of the RDI.

May I wish you happy and healthy eating. They go beautifully together.

Rosemary Stanton

CONTENTS

COOKERY RATING: easy   a little care needed

Why a Healthy Diet is Important

EVERYTHING IN YOUR BODY WAS ONCE IN YOUR FOOD. Feed yourself junk and you cannot expect your body to stay in top running order. On the other hand, if you feed your body well, it is likely to last longer and work better. Of course, there are exceptions. Most people know of someone who took little care of his or her body and lived to a ripe old age. On balance, however, most people who look after themselves live longer and are healthier throughout their longer lives than those who do not. Most important of all, they find that they feel better.

Creamy Salmon Pasta (page 46)

Some people believe a healthy diet takes the enjoyment away from eating. That is false. Most healthy foods also taste delicious. Think for a moment of the joy of sinking your teeth into a perfectly ripe peach or a lusciously juicy mango. Or remember the delights of a chunk of fragrant, freshly made wholemeal bread, or the simply perfect pleasure of eating some of our wonderful fresh seafoods.

The healthy choice

There are hundreds of examples of mouth-watering, healthy foods. In contrast, many of the foods which cause diet-related health problems are not always taste turn-ons. How many half-cold chips, soggy pastry cases, ordinary biscuits and gluggy sauces have you eaten – just because they were there? Many fat-laden foods and most of those bland processed and take-away foods are unremarkable and fail to live up to our preconceptions of their flavour. Most people eat these foods for convenience, not taste. Once your taste-buds experience the delights of fresh foods simply prepared and beautifully served, it is difficult to go back to eating many of the mundane offerings dished up relentlessly by some sections of the food industry.

Some foods are inherently delicious by virtue of their fat or salt or sugar and it is not always possible to make healthier versions of many of these goodies. There is no real substitute, for example, for good chocolate, rich creamy ice-creams and some wonderful, but fatty, cheeses. Some traditional recipes also cannot be changed without losing their essential character. But a healthy diet does not mean you should never have any of these indulgences. A well-balanced diet simply means eating more of some foods and less of others. And many recipes can be adapted to fit a healthier lifestyle without sacrificing their essential nature or taste.

It's true that some healthy foods do take a little more time and trouble to find and prepare. Does that matter? Is life worth such a rush that we forfeit the time we should devote to preparing for one of life's greatest pleasures – eating?

Setting appropriate limits

We all stop eating at some stage. Some people are good at setting appropriate limits; others are not.

Since we all set some type of limit on how much we eat, some foods need lower limits. Quality rather than quantity! To eat well and live longer, you may need to reset your limits on certain items. However, the many foods which are still delicious when prepared in a healthier way can become the mainstay of the diet. The occasional indulgence then does little harm. Just make sure your indulgences do not come too thick and fast, or your waistline will react the same way.

The balanced diet

As mentioned above, a balanced diet means eating more of some foods and a little less of others. This is easy with a three-step approach:

1 EAT MOST of fruits, vegetables, breads, cereals, grains, legumes and seafoods
2 EAT MODERATELY of chicken or turkey, lean meat, nuts, eggs and dairy products
3 EAT LEAST of sugar, fats, alcohol, salt.

Unfortunately, many people eat most from the EAT LEAST category and forget about the important foods such as breads, cereals, fruits and vegetables.

Fruits, vegetables, all foods made from grains, legumes and seafoods are all low in fat and provide a wide range of vitamins and minerals. All except the fruit and vegetables are important sources of protein and all except seafoods are valuable for their dietary fibre. Grains, breads, cereals and legumes, as well as fruits are all important suppliers of energy-giving carbohydrate.

Chicken or turkey, lean meat, nuts, seeds, eggs, milk, cheese and yoghurt are valuable for their protein, minerals and vitamins. All except dairy products are good sources of iron and zinc while dairy products earn a guernsey for their high calcium content. Although these foods all supply fats (in varying amounts), their fats accompany important nutrients. Nevertheless, they should be eaten in moderation and should not dominate the diet.

Apart from some fats such as olive oil, most fats, sugars, salt and alcohol are of little nutritional worth. Many processed and prepared foods have large amounts of fats and sugar. These are cheap 'filler' ingredients. In small quantities, these do

most people no harm. But, in the large quantities present in the average person's weekly shopping, they are known to cause health problems.

Changing the diet

Some people want to follow diets which others find extreme. Some of these are discussed in Alternative Diet Strategies at the end of this book. For most people, the risk of diet-related health problems can be reduced significantly by making a few small, simple changes to food choices.

Some people complain that the modern food supply lacks vitamins. That is not true. There are plenty of wonderfully nutritious foods with more than enough vitamins. Contrary to the cries of the scaremongers, there is no need to rush out and buy pills and expensive dietary supplements. Everything most people need can be found in food.

Cooking

Most people lead busy lives and there is often little time left for cooking. This is why so many take-away and highly processed foods are popular. It's not their taste that's the drawcard, it's the simplicity of buying a packet instead of having to plan a meal, do the shopping, cook and clean up afterwards. Many of these tasks traditionally have been left to women. Although many men are now doing some of these chores, surveys show that most food preparation is still done by women.

If we are to live longer, we have to go back to the kitchen. But not for hours and hours. There are many healthy meals and snacks which can easily be prepared in a minimum of time. And if all the family members share the tasks, preparing food can be a relaxing and enjoyable part of life rather than a chore consigned to one unfortunate person.

Top ten ticks for a healthy diet

- Feel on top of the world
- Plenty of energy for exercise or play
- Correct weight – not too high and not too low
- Blood fats (cholesterol and triglycerides) normal
- Blood sugar normal
- Strong bones
- Better able to cope with stress
- Reduced risk of many common health problems
- Immune system fighting fit
- Look younger

The Balanced Diet Pyramid

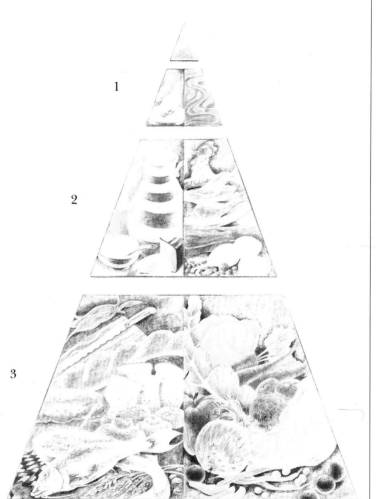

1 *Eat Least* — Sugar, Butter, Margarine, Oil

2 *Eat Moderately* — Meat, Chicken, Eggs, Nuts, Milk, Cheese, Yoghurt

3 *Eat Most* — Vegetables, Fruit, Bread, Cereals, Fish, Legumes

Diet-related Health Problems

More people are living longer than ever before. Much of the increase in life expectancy comes from conquering childhood diseases and infections. Women's life expectancy has increased dramatically with the advent of smaller families and safer childbirth. And the downturn in deaths from heart disease and strokes in middle-aged men is related to fewer men smoking, more men increasing their exercise and, probably, to changes in diet.

In many households, plate-sized fatty steaks and some saturated fats have disappeared from the dinner table and there is a conscious effort to eat less salt. Alcohol consumption is also dropping, more because of breathalyser tests than any health concerns. However, there are many small dietary changes which we could easily make to further decrease the risk of diet-related health problems.

Claims that pesticides and food additives are killing us are not supported by the facts. This does not mean we should relax our vigilance concerning these products but it does mean we do not need to avoid eating more fresh fruits and vegetables.

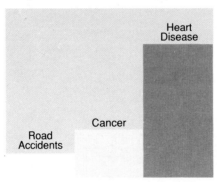

Heart disease. The major killer each year in Western society.

Diet and ageing
When most people think of the signs of ageing, they think of grey hair and facial wrinkles. In terms of health, these are relatively unimportant.

Factors such as unclogged arteries through which blood can flow unimpeded, a straight spine, firm muscles and brain cells which function well are much more important. And it is these factors which can be affected by diet and exercise. For those more interested in the cosmetics of ageing, it is worth noting that a stooped

spine and poor muscle tone may make us appear older than do a few grey hairs.

Naturally, all bodies age. None of us is immortal. But bodies that are uncared for, or abused with smoking, poor diet, little exercise and a lack of mental stimulation age much more rapidly.

Some people maintain that the effort of keeping the body fit and youthful is not worth the trouble. Eat, drink and be merry, they cry, assuming that one day they will simply drop dead. The reality is that the care you give your body is reflected in your health for many years before death. Some people do die of a sudden heart attack but many more suffer disabilities and restriction of their activities for 20 or 30 years prior to their death. On balance, those who care for their health when young have the last laugh as they age.

Extensive studies are being made into the effects of nutrition on delaying the ageing process. It has been known for some years that the way to extend the lifespan of rats is to restrict their food intake throughout life. Some scientists have recommended, therefore, that humans wanting to live longer should try semi-starvation rations of food. But humans do not have the same biochemistry as rats and recent long-term population studies in the Netherlands, Britain and Sweden have each found that people who eat more do live longer. There is a catch. The long-livers don't just eat more of anything; they specifically eat more of plant-based foods (grains, breads, cereals, legumes, fruits and vegetables) and more fish. They are not necessarily vegetarian, but they do not indulge heavily in animal products, with the possible exception of fish. With plant-based foods, you can eat more but not grow fat. You will also have a higher level of carbohydrates with which to fuel your muscles for exercise.

The ageing process in our internal tissues occurs because minute, highly reactive molecules – called free radicals – attack the body's cells. The free radicals are very unstable compounds and try to increase their own life by taking an electron from another molecule. In particular, they disrupt the polyunsaturated fats in the membranes around every body cell. These fats are easily oxidised and thus destroyed.

Factors such as radiation, cigarette

smoke, urban pollution, light, iron and copper as well as the presence of oxygen in tissues can all start free-radical reactions. Certain enzymes and antioxidant substances can prevent free-radical destruction of tissues. There is not much point in buying 'enzymes' from your health-food shop – there are hundreds of thousands of different enzymes which allow various chemical reactions to take place in the body. All enzymes are proteins and because enzyme supplements will be broken down by hydrochloric acid in the stomach, they will not reach individual cells.

However, the enzymes within the tissues which counter free-radical attack depend on a balanced supply of the minerals selenium, manganese, copper and zinc. It is important, therefore, to maintain a good balance of these substances in the daily diet. Too much of various minerals is as bad as or worse for you than too little, so high-dose supplements are not the answer to the problem. Some are useless; others are worse. Taking too much zinc, for example, can interfere with the body's absorption of iron and copper.

Vitamins A, C, E and, possibly vitamin K, are also important antioxidants. Whether taking supplements of these will help prevent free-radical reactions without doing any damage is still not known. All these vitamins can be harmful in excess.

The best method to combat the effects of free-radicals is to avoid cigarette smoke, to breathe air which is as clean as possible and also to have a diet which is rich in antioxidant vitamins and minerals. These are found in fruits and vegetables as well as wholegrain products.

Diet for anti-ageing
Eat more fruits and vegetables, wholegrain foods and fish. Eat some fruits and vegetables raw. Follow a balanced diet. Avoid too many fats, fried foods and salt. Be sure to include calcium-rich foods.

Coronary heart disease
Still the most common cause of death in Western countries, coronary heart disease is now becoming more common in some parts of Asia where people are forsaking their traditional diet of rice, vegetables, fish and fruit for the fatty 'pleasures' of the Western diet.

The major dietary problem for coronary heart disease is fat, especially saturated fat. Other important risk factors are cigarette smoking, excess weight on the upper body,

high blood pressure and lack of exercise. Women initially are protected from coronary heart disease by one of their hormones, oestrogen. After menopause, production of oestrogen slows down and women gradually acquire the same high risk of coronary heart disease as men. For young women, risk of heart disease is low; for older women the risk is as great as it is for men.

Coronary heart disease occurs gradually as fatty deposits accumulate in the arteries. The coronary arteries which supply the heart muscle with its vital blood supply are only the size of a drinking straw. Deposits of fat and fibrous material will narrow the area for blood flow, forcing the heart to work much harder.

It is best not to have fatty deposits develop in the first place but if it's too late for this warning, it is heartening to know that there is good evidence the situation can be made to regress with the adoption of a low-fat diet.

A blood test can determine your cholesterol level which, ideally, should be below 5.0 or 5.5 mmol/L. There is no point in becoming obsessed with reducing your level below about 4 mmol/L. Remember, too, that most blood cholesterol tests are only accurate to within about 10 per cent. Regular tests, as advised by your doctor, can give a good overall picture of what's happening in your arteries. Don't wait for symptoms – there will be none until the arteries are already clogged.

Levels of fats called triglycerides can also be measured; tests for both cholesterol and triglycerides are usually done at the same time. To measure triglyceride levels accurately, you need to have fasted for 12 hours; fasting is not needed for cholesterol measurements alone.

Diet to reduce high blood cholesterol

- Reduce weight to the healthy weight range with a balanced diet and moderate exercise such as walking, swimming or cycling
- Eat less fat, especially saturated fats
- Eat plenty of fibre-rich foods, especially those containing soluble fibre (oats, barley, beans, apples, vegetables)
- Eat fish one to three times a week
- For cooking, use only a very small amount of oil, preferably olive oil
- Make the time to learn some simple relaxation techniques.

Diet to reduce high triglycerides
- Reduce weight to normal with a low-fat diet and exercise
- Reduce all fats, especially saturated fats
- Keep sugar and alcohol intake to a minimum
- Eat more fish (fish-oil capsules may be required)

High blood pressure (also known as hypertension)

The heart pumps blood through the arteries to every tissue in the human body. Blood pressure refers to the strength with which blood pushes against the walls of the arteries.

If the arteries lose some of their elasticity – usually because hard, fatty deposits have built up on their walls – the heart must pump harder. And, if your body fat increases, the heart also has to pump harder to supply the additional tissue. When the diet is high in salt, extra fluid is retained in the body, forcing the heart to pump against a greater pressure. In addition, if the kidneys are not functioning properly – often because they have had to get rid of excess salt for many years – this places an increased strain on the heart and can send blood pressure soaring.

The upper reading of a blood-pressure measurement is the systolic pressure. It represents the pressure when the heart is contracting to force blood out through the arteries. The lower reading is the diastolic pressure and measures the pressure when the heart is relaxing between beats. Normal readings should not be greater than 120/80 mm of mercury. A higher level for the diastolic pressure is particularly dangerous as it means the heart is not getting its proper rest between beats.

Some people believe that high blood pressure is an inevitable part of ageing. However, primitive people in New Guinea and bushmen in parts of Africa register no increase in their blood pressure as they age. Both these groups consume a diet very low in salt, with no processed foods. Volunteers in many countries are currently following a low-salt diet to see if this can prevent the usual rise in pressure allied to age and, so far, results are very promising.

Smoking, stress and a lack of exercise are also significant adversaries. When the body is tense, small blood vessels constrict and blood pressure rises. Exercise keeps the arteries suitably elastic so that they do not harden.

Like salt, fats can contribute to high blood pressure, the saturated ones tending to stiffen or harden the arteries while monounsaturated or polyunsaturated ones do not. Fish fats can reduce pressure levels, possibly because they stop hard deposits forming on the artery walls.

Potassium and calcium may also give protection. Potassium helps to balance sodium (from salt) and is found in vegetables (especially potatoes, sweetcorn, spinach and pumpkin), fruits (prunes, rhubarb, melons, avocado and bananas), legumes, fish and milk. Calcium comes in dairy products and fish with edible bones (such as canned sardines or salmon).

Changing to a vegetarian diet can assist in the reduction of blood pressure; the reason for this is not yet known. But, since many people who do eat a balanced diet which includes moderate quantities of animal products do not have high readings, a vegetarian diet obviously is not essential. It is, however, an option.

High blood pressure tends to run in families. That does not mean it is inevitable and changes to diet, smoking, stress and exercise patterns can go a long way to prevent it ever developing.

All adults should have their blood pressure checked regularly as high levels can lead to strokes and heart failure.

To reduce high blood pressure
- If overweight, lose weight with a balanced diet and exercise (this is often the only treatment required)
- Eat less saturated fat
- Eat fish one to three times a week
- Don't use salt in cooking or at the table and choose unsalted food products where possible
- Eat foods rich in potassium to help balance the unavoidable sodium from salt
- Have plenty of calcium
- Walk, swim or regularly do some other moderate exercise
- Learn relaxation techniques

Note: Drugs may be required to control blood pressure. Most are effective at lower doses if you follow the dietary recommendations given, but consult your doctor.

Low blood pressure

This is not a disease; it is only a problem when blood pressure suddenly falls to a low level, as may occur after surgery or blood loss. Otherwise, low blood pressure is an inconvenience, not a condition which

requires that you undergo any treatment.

If your blood pressure is low, you may feel dizzy if you stand up quickly. The remedy is simply to stand up slowly. Eating less salt does not lower blood pressure in those with normal or low readings.

Osteoporosis

This condition arises when bones become porous and fragile and break easily. It occurs mainly in women, especially older women. Risk factors include the drop in female hormones after menopause or with extreme slimness, a lack of calcium in the diet, smoking and a lack of exercise.

Diet to avoid osteoporosis
- Plenty of calcium
- Avoid too much salt
- Stay within a healthy weight range, avoiding excessive slimness

Diabetes

There are two different types of diabetes: Type 1, or juvenile-onset diabetes and Type 2, or adult-onset diabetes. Type 1 diabetes occurs when the pancreas stops producing insulin, the hormone which normally takes glucose from the blood (blood sugar) into the cells where it can be used as a source of energy. If non-diabetics eat more sugar, they produce more insulin.

Type 1 diabetes does not seem to be caused by diet but adult-onset (responsible for about 95 per cent of all diabetes) is related to the quantity and quality of what we eat and drink. With this more common type, the pancreas may continue to produce insulin but the quantity may be insufficient or the action of the insulin may be blocked.

All carbohydrate foods are eventually digested to glucose. Some carbohydrates are broken down to glucose more quickly than others and may demand a large, sudden supply of insulin, while others take longer to be digested and absorbed. Soluble fibre in oats, barley, legumes and some fruits and vegetables slows down the rate at which glucose enters the blood and helps in the control of diabetes and fluctuating blood-sugar levels.

If you gain weight, your insulin supply does not increase. Adult-onset diabetes often occurs in overweight people because the body is producing only enough insulin for someone of normal weight. Once excess body fat is lost, the diabetes abates. A genetic factor must also be present.

Fats in the diet can cause cells to become resistant to the action of insulin. This 'insulin resistance' means that cells are starved of their major source of energy.

Whatever the underlying cause of diabetes, the effect is that glucose cannot get into the cells to provide energy. An untreated diabetic then feels excessively tired and lacking in energy. The glucose builds up in the blood and finally 'spills over' into the urine. A large volume of urine is passed and the untreated diabetic constantly feels thirsty. In some people, especially women, the frequent excretion of sweet urine can allow some bacteria to grow and cause an itch in the vulval area.

Children with Type I diabetes need insulin injections and will continue to need insulin throughout their life. Their dietary treatment requires the individual supervision of a dietitian. The diet will focus on foods which are high in carbohydrate and soluble fibre, avoid quickly absorbed carbohydrates such as sugar, unless present with fibre-containing foods, and provide enough kilojoules for growth and activity. Fatty foods should be avoided.

Diet for adult-onset diabetes
- Your doctor will advise if you need insulin or if diet is the main treatment
- Reduce weight to the limits of the healthy weight range, preferably keeping to the low side of the range
- Eat carbohydrate foods which are high in dietary fibre – wholemeal bread, wholegrain cereals (especially oats and barley), legumes, fruits and vegetables
- Divide food evenly throughout the day (a dietitian can help you plan this)
- Avoid fats, especially saturated fats
- Drink only in moderation, and never on an empty stomach
- Avoid sugar, except when present with high-fibre foods (a small serve of ice-cream occasionally is not usually a problem once weight is normal)

Cancer

Most research on the connections between diet and cancer has concentrated on cancers of the breast and bowel – two of the most common types in Western countries. The exact mechanisms relating a high-fat diet to these cancers are not fully understood but eating large amounts of fat does seem to create the right environment for cancer-causing substances (carcinogens) to gain a footing and cause cells to multiply at an abnormal rate.

Fat on the upper body is a factor in bowel cancer for both men and women, and is also related to a higher incidence of breast cancer in women over the age of 40.

Post-menopausal women who eat a high-fat diet have higher levels of hormone-related substances which are known to be cancer-forming. Dietary fat also causes a greater production of bile acids which can be converted to substances known to cause bowel cancer.

Dietary fibre may offer some protection against both breast and bowel cancers. Different types of fibre may be important in each of these conditions.

Soluble fibre seems to offer some protection against bowel cancer and starches in some foods such as rice may have a similar action. When bacteria in the large bowel digest soluble fibres, acids are formed. One of these, butyric acid, will inactivate an enzyme which bowel cancer cells need in order to multiply. Some types of starch also stimulate the production of these acids in the large bowel and this may help explain the low incidence of bowel cancer in most Asian people who eat their traditional diet. Bananas, cold potatoes and oats cooked and allowed to cool (as in the typical Scottish porridge oats) also contain this 'resistant starch'.

With breast cancer, insoluble fibres found in wholewheat or wheat-bran products change the bacterial population in the intestine and cause some carcinogens to be excreted.

There is also evidence that many types of cancer occur less in those who eat plenty of fruits and vegetables. This may be due to carotenes and/or vitamin C in these foods. Beta-carotene takes its name from 'carrots' which are one of the richest sources. All red, orange and green fruits and vegetables supply beta-carotene.

Vegetables and fruits rich in beta-carotene

Food	beta-carotene micrograms
Carrots, 100 g	12,000
Sweet potato, orange variety, 100 g	6780
Spinach, 100 g	6000
Mango, 1 medium	3800
Pumpkin, 100 g	3000
Rockmelon, dark-coloured, 150 g	3000
Broccoli, 100 g	2500
Apricots, dried, 50 g	1800
Capsicum, red, ½ medium	1500
Apricots, 3 medium	1500
Pawpaw, 150 g	1350
Dried peaches, 50 g	1000
Tomato, 1 medium	900

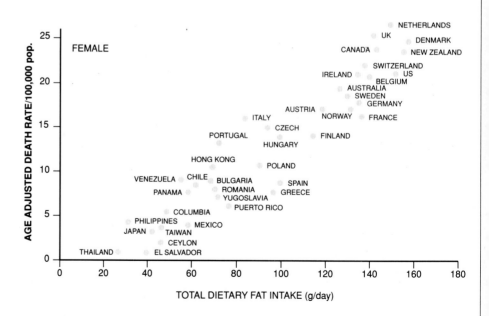

Dietary fat and the incidence of breast cancer

Vitamin C is found in all raw and lightly cooked vegetables (preferably that have been microwaved, steamed or stir-fried) and fruits. The richest sources of vitamin C include guavas, capsicum, broccoli, Brussels sprouts, pawpaw, citrus fruits, kiwi fruit, strawberries, cabbage, cauliflower, rockmelon, mango, peas, potatoes and tomatoes.

Diet for protection against cancer
- Eat less fat of all types
- Eat plenty of fruits and vegetables
- Eat plenty of wholegrain products, with as wide a variety as possible
- Eat more fish

Note: If you have any suspicion of cancer, always seek qualified medical treatment before any self-medication with diet.

Constipation and irritable bowel syndrome

Constipation is common, especially in women, and may become worse with age. It is usually caused by a lack of dietary fibre. Constipation also occurs in many children; it is less common in men. Irritable bowel syndrome, with alternating constipation and diarrhoea, may occur in men or women. Stress is an important factor and many people find their bowel reacts when they have to contend with any nervousness or stress.

The major factors involved in constipation include a lack of dietary fibre, a lack of water and, sometimes, insufficient exercise. Laxatives may work in the short term but are inadvisable. The main treatment for either constipation or irritable bowel syndrome is a high-fibre diet. However, see your doctor to make sure there are no major problems.

Diet to avoid or treat constipation
- Eat more fibre from a variety of sources (wholegrain cereals and cereal products, wholemeal bread, fruits, vegetables, seeds, nuts)
- Drink more water
- Avoid excessive amounts of finely milled, unprocessed bran

Gallstones

The gall-bladder is involved in the digestion of fat. Every time fat is present in the small intestine, the gall-bladder squirts out some bile to break it up. When the body is forced to process high levels of fat and make a lot of cholesterol, the gall-bladder becomes overworked and gallstones may form. The stones themselves consist to a large extent of cholesterol.

Diet for gallstones
- Reduce weight to normal with a low-fat diet and exercise
- Eat less of fats of all kinds
- Eat small amounts often rather than three large meals

Note: Always see your doctor if you suspect gallstones, as dietary treatment will not cure them.

Liver disease

All types of liver problems are potentially serious as the liver is a most complex organ and processes all the fats, proteins, carbohydrates and alcohol that we consume. The liver fortunately has enormous powers of regeneration. As soon as it ceases to function in the proper manner, you will usually feel nauseated and should seek medical attention.

Infections of the liver cause inflammations known as hepatitis. The organ may also develop fibrous areas caused by alcohol, even in those who would be classed as 'social' drinkers.

The nausea which accompanies most types of liver problems ensures that little fat is eaten. The fats in milk are usually well tolerated and a simple diet with milky drinks (skim, if needed) as well as fruits, vegetables, breads and cereals and fish, chicken or very lean meat is advisable. Avoid alcohol. Even after conditions such as hepatitis are over, it will take many months before the liver can cope with alcohol of any type.

Small, frequent meals are usually more appealing to anyone with liver disease than a large plate of food.

Weight

Excess weight is one of the major problems in our community. Being underweight can also be a problem. See the All About Weight section, page 106.

PRACTICALITIES OF LIVING ON A HEALTHY DIET

A healthy diet is a joy. We have a wonderful variety of foods available and healthy eating is simply a matter of making appropriate choices. But life in the healthy lane can sometimes appear difficult. So many foods seem to be loaded with fats, salt and sugar. And where is the dietary fibre in the fast foods, restaurant meals and prepared foods that line the freezer shelves of the supermarket?

Eating out

If you eat out only once or twice a year, it is not vitally important that all your choices be perfect. Exceptions to this occur for those with specific and dangerous food allergies and for diabetics.

For those who eat out more frequently, there are plenty of healthy choices available – if you know how to spot them. Here are some guidelines for avoiding fat and choosing the healthy foods in restaurants.

Choose seafoods. They not only taste wonderful, they are low in fat and kilojoules. Select oysters, prawns, lobster, crab, fish or any other seafood. All are low in fat – as long as they are not coated with batter or crumbs or served dripping with butter or a rich sauce. An oyster has about 50 kilojoules (12 Cals) and a good-sized prawn or a slice of smoked salmon weigh in at around 85 kJ (20 Cals). All have very little fat and are particularly low in saturated fat. Beware of battered or crumbed prawns – they can have eight times as many kilojoules as straight or barbecued prawns. Choose prawns with chilli sauce or a spicy Thai-style sauce but avoid mayonnaise and cream-based sauces. Ask for grilled seafoods to be prepared without butter.

Try game meats, if available. Venison and rabbit are very low in fat and are usually not served with cream sauces. Other lean meats include pork fillet, fillet steak or chicken breast. Veal has little fat but is usually served fried or in a rich sauce.

Choose any type of vegetables, either cooked or as salad but ask that cooked vegetables be served without butter and that salad dressings be 'on the side'. That way, you can add just a little for the flavour without having the salad drowned in fat.

Ask for plain bread rather than butter-soaked herb or garlic breads. If butter is served, resolve that you will skip it.

If you notice most meals being served with French fries, ask for yours to be served without. Or, ask for steamed potatoes.

Some sauces based on vegetable purées, wine or well-flavoured stocks are low in fat. Regrettably, many restaurants have a heavy-handed approach to sauces and load them with butter or cream. If in doubt, ask the waiter what sort of sauce is used, and ask for it to be served separately so you can add just a little.

Choose steamed rice rather than fried rice. Steamed rice not only goes better with most foods, it also has no fat.

Avoid cheese platters for dessert. Even the most sugary desserts have less fat than a hearty helping of cheese. Keep cheese consumption down to a small portion, and eat it at lunch with wholemeal bread, fruit and a salad rather than having it in place of a dessert.

If fresh fruit is available, ask for it to be served without cream. Most sorbets do not contain cream and are suitable for those wanting to avoid fat. They do contain sugar but they have only a fraction of the kilojoules of a rich ice-cream.

Pastry is one of the fattiest foods available. You can use filo pastry in some recipes and avoid fat, but this would be a rarity in restaurants.

Remember that you are paying for your meal and you are entitled to make reasonable requests for some items not to be served to you. Many waiters are more than happy to ask the chef to make minor adjustments to many of the dishes, providing you ask politely if this can be done. Be assertive but not aggressive.

Drinks

Most people use their first one or two drinks to quench their thirst. Do this by drinking one or two glasses of water before you move on to consuming any alcoholic or sugary drinks.

Recent research shows that sugary soft drinks are not effective in quenching thirst. Try water, mineral or soda water instead. Although some brands of mineral water once contained high levels of sodium, the amounts have now been reduced. If in doubt, read the label. Levels of sodium of 70 mg/L or less are not a problem for most people and this includes almost all brands of mineral water.

Ask waiters not to refill your wine glass until it is empty. This helps you know how many glasses of wine you have had – an important factor in avoiding exceeding the legal limit for alcohol as well as in looking after your waistline and triglyceride levels.

Entertaining

When you are hosting a party or lunch or dinner party, it is easy to serve healthy foods. There is no need to make a fuss about this; most people love well-prepared and interesting foods.

Some of the tips for entertaining are similar to those for eating at restaurants. You can use many of the recipes in this book. Here are some ways to make healthy eating a rewarding and enjoyable experience when entertaining.

Try to find foods you haven't eaten before. There's always something interesting at the fruit and vegetable shop – a new variety of lettuce or other salad vegetable, an exotic fruit, or something luscious such as fresh mangoes, raspberries or other berries. These foods might seem expensive but if you compare the cost of serving a bowl of beautiful summer berries with that of all the ingredients which go into making up many desserts, you will find the exotics cost less.

Try to give cheese and most crackers a miss. Apart from the rice variety, most crackers are high in fat and salt. In any case, these foods are always available so don't waste party choices on them. Serve some fresh vegetable crudités (snow peas, carrot sticks, celery, broccoli, cauliflower pieces, bright red capsicums) instead of crackers with a dip. Try pita bread with dips.

Use nuts as a garnish on vegetables or in main-course dishes rather than providing bowls of nuts for nibbling. Nuts are highly nutritious and are rich in dietary fibre, minerals and vitamins. They are also high in fats. Some, such as almonds, walnuts or pine nuts, have 'good' fats. All varieties of nut are high in kilojoules.

Serve seafoods, lean chicken, small pieces of very tender fillet steak, pork fillets or one of the recipes given in this book. For casual entertaining, some of the dishes in the Light Dishes section are ideal. Add some crusty bread and salad, then sit back and relax with your guests. Entertaining should be a pleasure for the hosts and their guests.

Use minimum quantities of salad dressings and intensify the flavour by using the stronger-flavoured oils such as extra virgin olive oil. Toss the salad gently so that the dressing just coats the ingredients instead of entirely drowning them.

Always serve mineral water as well as wine or beer. Light beer has far fewer kilojoules than regular beer. For mixed drinks, use low-kilojoule mixers.

Take-away tips

The best choices are grilled fish (most fish shops will grill fish if you ask); pizza (as long as you don't eat too much); pita or flat breads with salad (tabbouli, felafel, chicken); any salads; or grilled or barbecued chicken (remove the skin). Many places now have focaccia (Italian flat bread) or delicious, interesting rolls or breads stuffed with wonderful salad fillings. These are ideal for all healthy eaters. Also, remember that fresh fruit is the fastest food of all!

Adapting your favourite recipes

Many recipes can be adapted to have less fat, sugar and salt. Here are some helpful tips.

When sautéing onion in oil or butter, use a non-stick pan and heat it before adding the fat. Using this technique, you can reduce the oil or butter to less than half the usual level. You can also brush a pan with oil instead of pouring the oil into the pan.

Substitute low-fat yoghurt for sour cream in dips and some sauces. To stop yoghurt curdling, make sure it is at room temperature before use.

Stir-fry using a non-stick pan and concentrated chicken stock (made by boiling chicken stock until volume is reduced by half). You don't have to use fat.

Try using half the quantity of sugar in desserts and sweet sauces. (This does not always apply to cakes where the sugar is an integral part of the texture. Eat these types of cake in moderation.)

Use the same ingredients in a meal but change the balance. For example, have more vegetables and less meat.

Instead of using salt, add fresh or dried herbs, spices, a spoonful of lemon or lime juice. Use less water in vegetables and casseroles and you will lose less of the flavour from the original ingredients and so need less salt. Microwaving vegetables is the ideal way to preserve flavour.

Make up casseroles and soups ahead and chill in the refrigerator. It is then a very simple matter to remove all the fat which rises and solidifies on the top.

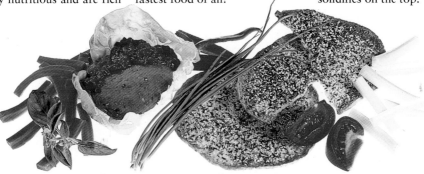

Satisfying Soups & Starters

WE TEND TO THINK OF SOUPS as cold-weather food, but here's a selection of recipes that will take you right through the seasons. Try hearty Veal and Vegetable on chilly days, and cooling Watercress Vichyssoise when the temperature starts to climb. The basis of a good soup is a good stock. It's well worth making the effort to prepare your own, and much easier than you might think. Many of these soups and starters can become light meals simply by adding a colourful, crisp salad and some crusty bread. For those planning a dinner party, select a special classic such as Sesame Prawns or Carpaccio of Salmon. Or, if something striking and a little unusual is what you're after, choose Pickled Vegetables with delicious crunchy Seeded Crispbread.

Fresh Tomato Soup (page 21) and Carpaccio of Salmon (page 26)

Creamy Cauliflower Soup

This basic soup recipe is a very good standby. By changing the vegetable and the accompanying herbs, you can have an amazing variety of light, yet filling and comforting soups – creamy, but without cream. Make sure you use a well-flavoured chicken stock.

PREPARATION TIME: *10 minutes*
COOKING TIME: *20 minutes (or 15 if using a microwave)*
SERVES 6

1 kg cauliflower, chopped roughly
4 cups chicken stock
1 medium onion, chopped roughly
3 bay leaves
sprig fresh mint
1 cup skim-milk powder
1 tablespoon snipped chives

1 Place all ingredients except milk powder and chives in a large saucepan. Bring to the boil and simmer 12-15 minutes, or until cauliflower is tender. Or microwave on High for 10 minutes.
2 Remove bay leaves and mint. Purée soup in food processor or blender, adding milk powder. Reheat. Serve in deep soup bowls and sprinkle with chives.

Nutritional information per serve:
Protein 11 g; no fat; carbohydrate 15 g; good dietary fibre 4 g; sodium 152 mg; 455 kJ (110 Cals)

Other features: An excellent source of vitamin C and niacin, a very good source of potassium and a good source of calcium. Also supplies some iron and B-complex vitamins

Black Bean Soup

Any leftovers of this wonderful dark soup can be frozen. Black beans are available from Asian food stores.

PREPARATION TIME: *10 minutes + soaking overnight*
COOKING TIME: *1 hour 20 minutes*
SERVES 6

Black Bean Soup

6 cups water
300 g black beans
6 cups chicken stock
2 chicken stock cubes
2 cloves garlic
1 teaspoon dried marjoram leaves
2 bay leaves
1 medium onion, diced
1 medium carrot, diced
2 small sticks celery, sliced
2 tablespoons tomato paste
1 teaspoon hot chilli sauce
1 tablespoon wine vinegar
2 tablespoons low-fat yoghurt
chilli powder

1 Soak beans in water overnight. Drain and discard water.
2 Cover beans with chicken stock, adding stock cubes, garlic, marjoram, bay leaves and vegetables. Bring to the boil and simmer 1 hour, or until beans are tender. Remove bay leaves.
3 Stir in tomato paste, chilli and vinegar. Serve with a swirl of low-fat yoghurt and a sprinkling of chilli powder.

Nutritional information per serve:
Protein 13 g; fat 1 g; carbohydrate 38 g; excellent dietary fibre 14 g; 730 kJ (175 Cals)

Other features: A very good source of iron and potassium, a good source of zinc and the B-complex vitamins. Also provides some calcium. Low sodium (100 mg)

Pumpkin and Rosemary Soup

This is a delicious soup, simple and fast to make. Cut the pumpkin in small pieces to reduce cooking time.

PREPARATION TIME: *15 minutes*
COOKING TIME: *20 minutes (or 12-15 in a microwave)*
SERVES 6

1 kg pumpkin flesh
4 cups chicken stock
3 sprigs rosemary (or use 1 teaspoon dried rosemary leaves)
3 bay leaves
1 cup skim-milk powder

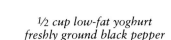

½ cup low-fat yoghurt
freshly ground black pepper

1 In a large saucepan, combine pumpkin, stock and herbs. Bring to the boil, cover and simmer for about 15 minutes or until pumpkin is cooked. Remove rosemary sprigs and bay leaves.
2 Purée soup, adding skim-milk powder. Serve in bowls, top each with a spoonful of yoghurt and a sprinkle of black pepper. Garnish with a sprig of fresh rosemary.

Nutritional information per serve:
Protein 11 g; fat 2 g; carbohydrate 23 g; good dietary fibre 3 g; sodium 140 mg; 525 kJ (125 Cals)

Other features: A very good source of calcium and potassium, a good source of vitamins A and C and provides some iron and zinc

Mushroom Soup

Large, dark field mushrooms give an intense flavour to mushroom soup. If they are unavailable, large flat mushrooms are a good substitute.

PREPARATION TIME: *10 minutes*
COOKING TIME: *30 minutes*
SERVES 4

2 teaspoons butter or margarine
1 medium onion, diced
1 teaspoon French mustard
1 teaspoon dried thyme leaves
500 g mushrooms, preferably field or
flat, chopped roughly
3 cups chicken or veal stock
½ cup red wine
1 tablespoon sour light cream
few sprigs thyme

1 Heat butter in a saucepan and gently cook onion for 3-4 minutes, allowing it to brown slightly.
2 Add mustard, thyme and mushrooms and cook a further 2-3 minutes, stirring gently.
3 Add stock and wine, bring to the boil, cover and simmer for 10 minutes. Purée soup. Serve with a drizzle of sour cream on top of each bowl. Garnish with a sprig of fresh thyme.

Nutritional information per serve:
Protein 6 g; fat 4 g; carbohydrate 5 g; very good dietary fibre 4 g; 295 kJ (70 Cals)

Other features: A very good source of riboflavin and niacin and a good source of potassium. Low sodium (80 mg)

Fresh Tomato Soup

The secret of making a good tomato soup is to use very ripe tomatoes and a well-flavoured stock. Sieve the soup and you won't need to peel the tomatoes.

PREPARATION TIME: *10 minutes*
COOKING TIME: *30 minutes*
SERVES 6

2 teaspoons olive oil
1 medium onion, diced
1 clove garlic, crushed
1 teaspoon sugar
½ teaspoon chopped chilli (optional)
1 kg ripe tomatoes, chopped roughly
1 tablespoon tomato paste (no
added salt)
3 cups veal or chicken stock
bunch fresh herbs (try parsley, basil or
thyme, mint and rosemary)
freshly ground pepper

1 Heat oil, add onion and garlic, cover and cook over a gentle heat for 3-4 minutes.
2 Add sugar, chilli, tomatoes and tomato paste and stir well. Cook for a further 2-3 minutes. Add stock and herbs, bring to the boil, cover and simmer for 10 minutes (do not overcook).
3 Remove herbs. Purée soup, then rub through a sieve to remove any pieces of tomato skin. Add pepper to taste.

Nutritional information per serve:
Protein 3 g; fat 2 g; carbohydrate 10 g; good dietary fibre 3 g; 295 kJ (70 Cals)

Other features: An excellent source of vitamin C, a good source of niacin and potassium and has useful amounts of iron and vitamin A. Low sodium (40 mg)

Most brands of cornflour contain added wheat starch and are unsuitable for people on gluten-free diets. Arrowroot and cornflour can be interchanged in most recipes. Arrowroot gives a clearer thickening and is often used in lemon sauces for this reason.

Back: Veal and Vegetable Soup. Front: Mushroom Soup (page 21)

Veal and Vegetable Soup

This is one of those hearty soups which becomes a meal in itself. Make it on a weekend and freeze it to use as an ideal standby in winter. By freezing individual serves it is very easy to defrost and heat a nourishing meal in the microwave in a matter of minutes.

PREPARATION TIME: *30 minutes*
COOKING TIME: *2 hours*
SERVES 6

1 tablespoon butter or margarine
1 large onion, sliced
1 clove garlic
1 veal knuckle (ask butcher to saw it through)
1½ litres water
1 teaspoon mixed dried herbs
½ cup split peas
½ cup pearl barley
1 large potato, peeled and diced
1 bulb kohlrabi, peeled and diced
1 leek, washed and sliced
1 large carrot, diced
1 large parsnip, peeled and diced
1 stalk celery, sliced
1 cup sliced green beans (or broccoli pieces)
1 cup sliced mushrooms
1 tablespoon chopped parsley

1 Melt butter or margarine and gently cook onion and garlic for 3-4 minutes. Add veal and cook 3-4 minutes longer, stirring occasionally.
2 Add water, herbs, peas and barley, bring to the boil, cover and simmer for 1½ hours.
3 Add potato, kohlrabi, leek, carrot and parsnip and cook for a further 20 minutes. Remove veal.
4 Add celery, beans and mushrooms to soup and simmer a further 10 minutes.
5 While vegetables are cooking, remove meat from veal bone and return meat to soup. Serve topped with parsley.

Nutritional information per serve:
Protein 25 g; fat 4 g; carbohydrate 29 g; excellent dietary fibre 8 g; sodium 140 mg; 1050 kJ (250 Cals)

Other features: A very good source of niacin, riboflavin, potassium and vitamin A and a good source of thiamin, zinc, iron and vitamin C

Chilled Tomato Soup

This richly flavoured soup is a delightful summer starter. Make sure you use rich, red, ripe tomatoes, sometimes sold as cooking tomatoes.

PREPARATION TIME: *20 minutes*
+ 2 hours chilling time
COOKING TIME: *Nil*
SERVES 4

1 kg rich, ripe, red tomatoes, cored
2 medium cucumbers
1 small onion
1 medium red capsicum
2 cloves garlic, crushed
1 cup beef stock
few sprigs thyme
2 tablespoons chopped parsley
1 tablespoon lemon juice
freshly ground pepper

1 Skin tomatoes by covering with boiling water for 1 minute then plunging them into iced water. Dice finely.
2 Cut cucumbers lengthwise and remove seeds. Dice flesh finely. Dice onion and capsicum finely (some food processors do this well). Combine with tomatoes, garlic, beef stock and thyme. Leave to stand for at least 2 hours for flavours to blend. Remove thyme.
3 Add parsley and lemon juice just before serving. Add freshly ground pepper to taste. Float an ice-cube on top of soup in each bowl.

Nutritional information per serve:
Protein 5 g; no fat; carbohydrate 12 g; very good dietary fibre 5 g; 275 kJ (65 Cals)

Other features: An excellent source of vitamin C, a very good source of potassium and a good source of vitamin A and niacin. Also provides riboflavin and iron. Low sodium (45 mg)

Do not soak potatoes and other vegetables before cooking as they lose large amounts of vitamin C. Green capsicums are a rich source of vitamin C but red capsicums are even better. Kale is a member of the cabbage family. It is very rich in vitamin C and contains substances which may give protection against cancer.

Watercress Vichyssoise

A refreshing but filling summer soup. Serve with some fresh crusty bread and follow with fresh fruit for a superb lunch.

PREPARATION TIME: *15 minutes*
COOKING TIME: *30 minutes + 2 hours chilling time*
SERVES 4

2 teaspoons butter or margarine
1 medium onion, chopped roughly
2 medium leeks, washed and sliced
2 large potatoes, peeled and sliced
4 cups chicken stock
3 bay leaves
1 teaspoon finely grated lemon rind
1 bunch watercress, washed
200 g low-fat yoghurt
few sprigs thyme

1 Heat butter, add onion, cover. Gently sweat onion for 3-4 minutes.
2 Add leeks, potato, stock, bay leaves and rind, simmer for 15 minutes.
3 Remove coarse stems from watercress and add the leaves to saucepan. Cook 2 minutes. Remove bay leaves. Cool.
4 Purée soup, swirl in yoghurt and chill until ready to serve. Garnish each serve with a sprig of thyme.

Nutritional information per serve:
Protein 8 g; fat 3 g; carbohydrate 20 g; very good dietary fibre 5 g; 595 kJ (140 Cals)

Other features: An excellent source of vitamin C, a very good source of potassium and a good source of iron, vitamin A, riboflavin and niacin. Also a useful source of calcium. Low sodium (120 mg)

It takes 2-3 months for the average person's taste-buds to adjust to less salt. Give up gradually and you will have no trouble adjusting to the new-found natural flavours in foods. To reduce the salt in feta cheese, hold the amount you are going to use that day under the tap for a few minutes. Pat dry with paper towels.

Carrot and Orange Soup

PREPARATION TIME: *15 minutes*
COOKING TIME: *30 minutes*
SERVES 4

500 g carrots, sliced
1 large potato, peeled and sliced
2 cups chicken stock

1 cup orange juice
1 teaspoon chopped fresh ginger
1 teaspoon curry powder

Combine all ingredients, bring to the boil, cover and simmer for 20 minutes, or until vegetables are tender. Purée until smooth. Serve the soup garnished with yoghurt and dill, if desired.

Nutritional information per serve:
Protein 3 g; no fat; carbohydrate 19 g; very good dietary fibre 5 g; 380 kJ (90 Cals)

Other features: An excellent source of vitamins A and C, a good source of niacin and potassium. Also provides useful amounts of iron. Low sodium (90 mg)

Chicken Stock

Buy chicken bones or a boiling fowl to make your own chicken stock, the result is far superior to purchased stock cubes. You can purchase chicken bones from a poultry shop or freeze bones from chicken dishes until you have about a kilogram.

PREPARATION TIME: *10 minutes*
COOKING TIME: *1½-2 hours*
MAKES *1 litre*

1 kg chicken bones or 1 boiling fowl
2 litres water
1 medium onion, chopped roughly
2 bay leaves
8-10 peppercorns
1 small stalk celery, chopped roughly
1 small carrot, chopped roughly
few pieces fresh parsley or thyme

1 Place all ingredients in a large saucepan, bring to the boil, cover, simmer for 1-1½ hours, or microwave, covered, on High for 40 minutes. Strain, then cool and refrigerate.
2 Remove any fat from top. Freeze if desired.
3 Chicken stock can be reduced by boiling rapidly without a lid until ⅔ volume remains. (Reduced chicken stock is ideal for stir-frying vegetables.) Freeze if desired.

Nutritional information per serve:
1 cup chicken stock has 75 kJ (18 Cals)

Watercress Vichyssoise and Scandinavian Fruit Soup

Scandinavian Fruit Soup

The palate never tires of the fresh flavour of this soup. Serve it hot or chilled, as a starter, for a light lunch, a dessert, breakfast or a delicious supper.

PREPARATION TIME: *5 minutes + at least 1 hour soaking*
COOKING TIME: *30 minutes + 2 hours refrigeration if served cold*
SERVES 6

500 mL apple juice
500 mL orange juice
1 cup dried apricots
½ cup dried apples
½ cup raising
1 piece cinnamon stick, about 6 cm long
3 or 4 cardamon pods
½ cup sago
½ cup low-fat yoghurt
½ teaspoon finely grated orange rind

1 Place juices, fruit, spices and sago in a large saucepan and leave to soak for at least 1 hour.
2 Bring mixture to the boil, simmer gently for 15 minutes. Remove cinnamon stick and cardamom pods. If serving cold, cool and then refrigerate for at least 2 hours. Serve topped with a swirl of yoghurt and a sprinkle of orange rind.

Nutritional information per serve:
Protein 3 g; no fat; carbohydrate 52 g; excellent dietary fibre 9 g; 920 kJ (220 Cals)
Other features: A very good source of potassium. Provides some calcium. Low sodium (70 mg)

Pickled Vegetables

Bought pickled vegetables are usually high in salt. Why not try making your own?

PREPARATION TIME: *30 minutes + 1 week standing time*
COOKING TIME: *Nil*
MAKES 1½ L

1 large carrot, peeled, cut into 10 cm strips
200 g small onions
1 cup cauliflower pieces
2 medium zucchini, cut into 10 cm strips
1 red capsicum, seeded, cut into 10 cm strips
1 green capsicum, seeded, cut into 10 cm strips
600 mL wine vinegar
2 teaspoons mustard seeds
10 peppercorns
4 cloves

1 Steam carrot, onions and cauliflower for 3 minutes or microwave, covered, on High for 1½ minutes. Drain.
2 Pour boiling water into a 1½ litre jar. Drain.
3 Arrange all vegetables in sterilised jar.
4 Combine vinegar with mustard, peppercorns and cloves. Pour over vegetables, making sure vegetables are completely covered in vinegar. Seal and leave in refrigerator at least a week before use.

Nutritional information per serve:
Protein 2 g; no fat; carbohydrate 4 g; some dietary fibre 2 g; 105 kJ (25 Cals)

Other features: Provides some potassium. Low sodium (15 mg)

Seeded Crispbread

PREPARATION TIME: *10 minutes*
COOKING TIME: *8 minutes*
SERVES 4-8

4 wholemeal pita breads
1 egg white
2 tablespoons water
2 tablespoons sesame seeds
2 tablespoons poppy seeds
1 tablespoon fennel seeds

1 Carefully separate pita bread and lay each piece out flat.
2 Using a fork, beat egg white and water.
3 Using a pastry brush, brush surface of pita bread with egg-white mixture and sprinkle with seeds. Bake on oven shelf at 180°C until crisp (7-8 minutes), taking care not to burn. Break into pieces to serve with Salmon Mousse or any dip.

Nutritional information per serve:
Protein 6 g; fat 5 g; carbohydrate 13 g; some dietary fibre 3 g; sodium 165 mg; 485 kJ (115 Cals)

Other features: Provides some B-complex vitamins, vitamin E, iron and zinc

Carpaccio of Salmon

One of the simplest and most delicious starters, this can be prepared in minutes. Served with a good rye bread and a salad of different lettuce leaves, it is also an excellent lunch dish.

PREPARATION TIME: *10 minutes + 30 minutes for freezing the salmon*
COOKING TIME: *Nil*
SERVES 4

200 g piece of fresh salmon
lettuce, preferably butterhead or cabbage
1 head witloof
freshly ground black pepper
1½ tablespoons extra virgin olive oil
1 tablespoon lime juice (or use lemon)
1 tablespoon fresh basil leaves, shredded (optional)

1 Place salmon in freezer for 30 minutes. Remove and slice very thinly.
2 Arrange lettuce leaves and witloof to one side of each plate. Spread salmon slices over remainder of plate and sprinkle with plenty of freshly ground pepper.
3 Combine olive oil and lime juice. Sprinkle over salmon and strew with basil, if desired.

Nutritional information per serve:
Protein 11 g; fat 7 g; no carbohydrate; dietary fibre 1 g; 460 kJ (110 Cals)

Other features: A useful source of potassium. Low sodium (80 mg)

The Mediterranean diet (fish, vegetables, fruits, olive oil and almonds plus small amounts of yoghurt and cheese) leads to a long, healthy life.

Clockwise from top: Pickled Vegetables, Grilled Eggplant (page 28) and Seeded Crispbread

Nutty Spread

Delicious on wholemeal toast, or with Lebanese bread (fresh or baked until crisp). Also great on top of a steamed potato in its jacket.

PREPARATION TIME: *5 minutes + at least 1 hour standing time*
COOKING TIME: *10 minutes*
MAKES *1 cup*

> Always eat a tomato or some other food source of vitamin C with smoked and salted foods. Vitamin C eaten with these foods stops the nitrites in the food from forming cancer-causing nitrosamines in the stomach.

2 teaspoons ground cumin
1 teaspoon ground coriander
1 tablespoon chopped spring onions
2 slices wholemeal bread
½ teaspoon cinnamon
2 tablespoons lemon juice
2 teaspoons olive oil

1 Gently cook cumin and coriander in a dry frying pan for 2-3 minutes, taking care spices do not burn.
2 Place all ingredients in a food processor and blend until smooth.
3 Pack into a small bowl and leave to stand for at least an hour before serving.

Nutritional information per tablespoon:
Protein 3 g; fat 6 g; carbohydrate 4 g; some dietary fibre 2 g; low sodium 36 mg; 350 kJ (85 Cals)

Grilled Eggplant

This is an excellent starter or light lunch. It is well flavoured and is an ideal first course before a pasta dish or a barbecue.

PREPARATION TIME: *10 minutes + 30 minutes standing time*
COOKING TIME: *10 minutes*
SERVES 4

2 small eggplants (about 300 g each)
1 teaspoon sesame oil
1 teaspoon olive oil
freshly ground black pepper
2 tablespoons sesame seeds
4 small tomatoes
1 tablespoon chopped fresh basil

1 Slice eggplant. Combine oils and pepper and warm slightly (30 seconds in a microwave is ideal). Brush the eggplant

slices with oil. Cover and leave for at least 30 minutes.
2 Place eggplant on foil-lined griller tray and grill until brown (about 5 minutes).
3 Turn eggplant slices, sprinkle with sesame seeds and grill again until brown (take care sesame seeds do not burn).
4 Slice tomatoes and place on flat dish with eggplant. Sprinkle with basil and serve warm with focaccia or other bread.

Nutritional information per serve (without bread):
Protein 4 g; fat 6 g; carbohydrate 6 g; very good dietary fibre 5 g; 360 kJ (85 Cals)

Other features: An excellent source of vitamin C, a good source of potassium and provides some niacin, vitamin A and iron. Low sodium (10 mg)

Cucumber Salad

An ideal starter to serve before curries. The cucumber is salted to give it the right texture but the final salt content is not high as the salt is rinsed away.

PREPARATION TIME: *10 minutes + 30 minutes standing time*
COOKING TIME: *Nil*
SERVES 4

2 medium cucumbers, about 250 g each
1 teaspoon salt
1 tablespoon finely chopped mint
½ cup low-fat yoghurt
freshly ground pepper

1 Peel cucumbers, cut them in half lengthwise and remove the seeds (use a teaspoon). Slice cucumber flesh thinly and place on a plate. Sprinkle with salt and leave for 20-30 minutes.
2 Rinse cucumber, drain well, and gently squeeze out any moisture.
3 Toss together cucumber, mint, yoghurt and a good grinding of pepper. Serve within 30 minutes.

Nutritional information per serve:
Protein 2 g; no fat; carbohydrate 5 g; dietary fibre 1 g; 125 kJ (30 Cals)

Other features: A good source of vitamin C. Low sodium (50 mg)

Salmon Mousse

This dish can be served with bread and salad for lunch or a light evening meal.

PREPARATION TIME: *15 minutes + 2 hours setting time*
COOKING TIME: *Nil*
SERVES *4*

¾ cup ricotta cheese (low-fat)
⅓ cup evaporated skim-milk
1 teaspoon paprika
½ cup fresh coriander
¼ cup sliced spring onions
220 g can red salmon, drained
1 tablespoon gelatine
2 tablespoons lemon juice
¼ cup boiling water
2 egg whites

1 Place ricotta, evaporated milk, paprika and coriander in blender and process until smooth and creamy. Fold in spring onions and salmon.
2 Soften gelatine in lemon juice, dissolve in ¼ cup boiling water. Stir into salmon mixture.
3 Beat egg whites until stiff and fold into salmon. Place in 4 x ½ cup capacity wet moulds and refrigerate until set. Mousse may be flaked with a fork to serve. Serve with Seeded Crispbread and a salad.

Nutritional information per serve:
Protein 21 g; fat 7 g; carbohydrate 4 g; no dietary fibre; sodium 445 mg; 710 kJ (170 Cals)

Other features: A very good source of niacin and riboflavin, a good source of calcium and provides some iron, zinc, potassium and vitamin A

1 Place ricotta, evaporated milk, paprika and coriander in processor, process until smooth.

2 Carefully fold drained and flaked salmon and spring onions into ricotta mixture.

3 Stir dissolved gelatine and water into salmon mixture.

Roquefort cheese is made from sheep's milk. Sheep's milk has a higher fat content than cow's milk. The lower the fat level of mozzarella cheese, the more stringy it is when used as a pizza topping. Sour light cream has 18 per cent fat – about half the level of regular sour cream.

Roasted Eggplant and Red Capsicum Dip; Sesame Prawns

Sesame Prawns

Now that researchers have finally confirmed that eating prawns does not raise cholesterol, we can all indulge in these wonderful crustaceans with a clear conscience. Just 2 or 3 of these sesame prawns make an ideal starter.

PREPARATION TIME: *20 minutes (or 10 minutes if using peeled prawns) + 30 minutes for marinating*
COOKING TIME: *3 minutes*
SERVES 4

1 tablespoon salt-reduced soy sauce
1 tablespoon sherry
1 teaspoon sesame oil
2 teaspoons chopped fresh ginger
1 clove garlic, crushed
12 large green prawns, peeled, but with the tail left on
2 tablespoons sesame seeds

1 Combine soy sauce, sherry, oil, ginger and garlic. Add prawns, cover and refrigerate for 30 minutes.
2 Remove prawns from marinade and thread on to small bamboo skewers (soaked in water to prevent burning). Roll prawns in sesame seeds and grill or barbecue for about 3 minutes.

Nutritional information per serve:
Protein 19 g; fat 6 g; carbohydrate 1 g; dietary fibre 1 g; sodium 445 mg 545 kJ (130 Cals)

Other features: A good source of iodine, and provides some iron, zinc, calcium and B-complex vitamins

Carrot and Orange Soup (page 24)

Roasted Eggplant and Red Capsicum Dip

Removing the skin from red capsicums gives a deliciously sweet flavour. It is well worth the effort.

PREPARATION TIME: 50 minutes
COOKING TIME: *Nil*
SERVES 6

1 eggplant, about 450 g
2 red capsicums
2 cloves garlic, crushed
1 teaspoon coriander seeds
2 tablespoons lemon juice
1 tablespoon extra virgin olive oil
1/2 teaspoon paprika
1 tablespoon chopped parsley

1 Place eggplant on oven shelf and bake at 180°C for 30 minutes.
2 While eggplant is roasting, skin capsicums; halve them and place, skin side up, under a grill and cook until blackened. Wrap blackened capsicums in a clean damp cloth or tea towel and leave for about 10 minutes. Skin will then rub off.
3 Place coriander seeds in a saucepan, cover and heat until they begin to pop (do not burn).
4 In blender, combine eggplant flesh (discard skin), capsicums (discard seeds), garlic, coriander and lemon juice. Process until smooth. Pour into a serving dish. Combine olive oil and paprika and drizzle it over the top. Sprinkle with chopped parsley.

Nutritional information per serve:
Protein 2 g; fat 4 g; carbohydrate 5 g; good dietary fibre 3 g; 275 kJ (65 Cals)

Other features: An excellent source of vitamin C. Negligible sodium (8 mg)

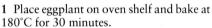

Grapeseed oil is a polyunsaturated oil, like safflower, sunflower or corn oil. Olive oil is the preferred oil. Try using extra virgin olive oil on salads. Its strong flavour means you use less. If salad greens are dry, less dressing is needed.

ALL ABOUT FAT

Almost everyone thinks previous generations ate much more fat with breakfasts of sausages, bacon and fried eggs and roast dinners followed by apple pie and cream. In fact, people in most Western countries today eat more fat than their predecessors, the major difference being that it is now concealed in fast foods, processed and take-away items.

Is fat essential?
Babies begin life drinking breast or formula milks in which 50 per cent of the kilojoules come from fat. This is important for a baby's rapid growth, and, for the first few years of life, dietary fat continues to be an important source of energy. Gradually, however, the need for fat decreases.

Everyone needs some essential fatty acids. You won't find these in fatty meats, pastries, chips or most fried foods. Essential fatty acids are in many foods without any obvious fat. Rabbit, turkey, chicken, fish, rolled oats, wheatgerm, egg yolk, nuts, seeds and vegetables are all sources of the essential fatty acids needed by brain and nerve cells and to keep the membranes around all body cells healthy. Many vegetable oils also contain essential fatty acids.

Why too much fat is harmful
A high fat diet is linked with excess weight, coronary heart disease and high blood pressure, diabetes, gallstones and some cancers. At 37 kilojoules/gram, fats have more than twice as many kilojoules as protein (17 kJ/g) or carbohydrates (16 kJ/g). Only alcohol, with 29 kJ/g comes close to fat in kilojoules.

To damn fat further, researchers have now shown that the body preferentially uses carbohydrates for energy and more easily converts fats in food into body fat. High levels of body fat then further increase the risks for all the conditions listed above.

Western diseases
In countries where the diet is low in fat, there is a very small incidence of 'Western diseases'. However, when people migrate, they pick up the host country's pattern of disease. When Japanese people move to the United States, they develop problems associated with a high fat diet such as heart disease, diabetes, gallstones, and cancers of the breast and bowel.

Eating saturated fat can cause the body to make too much cholesterol. This occurs more in some people than in others.

Excess dietary fat also increases the load on the heart so it must pump much harder. This can cause blood pressure to rise. Saturated fats create the greatest risk for high blood pressure. Saturated fats are also a risk factor in maturity-onset diabetes. For gallstones, all fats are a problem. In certain cancers, too much of any kind of fat – except for fish fats, and monounsaturated fat present in olive oil – is also a potential problem.

Different kinds of fat – saturated or unsaturated?
'Saturated', 'monounsaturated' and 'polyunsaturated' refer to the chemical structure of fats. Foods always contain a mixture of many different fats but one type usually predominates. For example, a margarine which is labelled 'polyunsaturated' may have 45 per cent of its fat in the form of polyunsaturated fat, 35 per cent as monounsaturated fat and 20 per cent as saturated fat. Even polyunsaturated margarines thus contribute some saturated fat to the diet - a point which often escapes notice.

Some types of fat create more health problems than others. People living in Mediterranean countries eat a lot of olive oil but have long life expectancy with low levels of heart disease and cancer. Traditional Eskimos also

Major types of fat in different foods

Food	Sat fat	Mono fat	Poly fat
	g	g	g
Milk, 200 mL glass	5	5	0
Butter, 1 tablespoon	10	5	0
Margarine, 1 tablespoon	6	8	1
Polyunsaturated margarine, 1 tablespoon	2	6	7
Olive oil, 1 tablespoon	3	14	2
Sunflower oil, 1 tablespoon	3	6	10
Palm kernel oil, 1 tablespoon	9	9	2
Coconut oil, 1 tablespoon	18	1	0
Dripping, 1 tablespoon	9	10	1
Beef, grilled, lean, 150 g	6	6	<1
Chicken breast, cooked, 150 g	1	2	1
Pork, steak, cooked, lean, 150 g	3	3	1
Lamb, trimmed, cooked, 150 g	7	5	0
Fish, grilled, 150 g	1	1	1

had very low levels of heart disease, diabetes and many other health problems, even though their diet was high in fat. Their secret lay in fish fats. The high content of saturated fats in the typical Western diet seems to be responsible for many of our diet-related health problems.

Animal or vegetable fats?
Saturated fats are not synonymous with animal fats. Some animal fats, such as those in fish and game meats (like venison) are mainly unsaturated. On the other hand, many vegetable fats, such as those found in chocolate, some margarines, coconut and palm kernel oils are highly saturated fats. When a food product lists 'vegetable oil' on its label, the ingredient is often palm kernel oil - a highly saturated fat.

Some saturated fats affect blood cholesterol more than others. Claims are sometimes made that chocolate contains stearic acid. This is a saturated fat which does not seem to raise cholesterol. However, chocolate is also one of the richest sources of palmitic acid - a saturated fat which does indeed raise blood cholesterol levels.

Which fat?
There is little doubt that saturated fats are undesirable while the monounsaturated ones are better, as shown by the long, healthy lifespan of those who eat a lot of olive oil. We know less about the polyunsaturated fats as they have been consumed in large quantities only since the 1970s.

The best advice for a longer life is to cut back on all fats, especially saturated fats, and use monounsaturated fats like olive oil instead.

Cholesterol
Cholesterol is essential in small quantities for brain and nerve cells and for hormones. Some cholesterol comes ready-made in animal foods but most is made in the body. It is the body's excess synthesis of cholesterol which causes problems. When the diet is high in saturated fats, more cholesterol is made. Excess cholesterol in the blood leads to clogged arteries, especially the arteries to the heart and brain. Cholesterol can also block blood vessels to the penis and is the major physical cause of impotence in men.

Cholesterol is made up of both HDL cholesterol (high density lipoprotein) and LDL cholesterol (low density lipoprotein). HDL cholesterol is 'good' and represents cholesterol being taken back from the tissues to the liver. LDL cholesterol is 'bad' and correlates with fatty deposits in the arteries.

Ideally, blood cholesterol levels should be less than 5.0-5.5 mmol/L. The higher the percentage of HDL cholesterol the better. Those from long-lived families, young women and endurance athletes tend to have high HDL cholesterol levels, generally ranging from 25 to 40 per cent of the total. Most men and most post-menopausal women have HDL levels less than 20 per cent of the total.

How to lower your cholesterol
Saturated fats lower protective HDL cholesterol and increase the nasty LDL type. Polyunsaturated fats reduce the bad LDL cholesterol and are preferable to saturated fats. Monounsaturated fats can reduce the bad LDL cholesterol and may raise the good HDL cholesterol. These fats are therefore best. They are found in olive or canola oils, avocado and nuts such as almonds.

In trying to reduce blood cholesterol, many people make the mistake of avoiding foods which contain cholesterol (such as eggs) while continuing to eat foods which contain saturated fats. For example, changing from animal fats to vegetable fats may not reduce your intake of saturated fat if the vegetable fat is still saturated, as many are. The best way to reduce your blood cholesterol is to avoid saturated fats and lose any excess weight. Stress can also be a factor in raising blood cholesterol levels.

Triglycerides
We convert excess fats, alcohol and sugar into triglycerides. After a meal, the level of triglycerides in the blood rises. Those not used for energy are tucked away in fat depots. If the blood level of triglycerides is still high after a 12-hour fast, it shows the body is not clearing fats properly. This may occur in those with a predisposition to diabetes. High triglyceride levels mean the blood is fatty and the heart must work harder.

Fish fats
The small quantity of fat in most fish is rich in omega 3 fatty acids. These are chemically different from the omega 6 fatty acids in margarines and many varieties of vegetable oils.

The omega 3 fatty acids can prevent blood clots forming, make blood less 'sticky', lower blood pressure and triglyceride levels, and can play a role in reducing inflammation in some kinds of arthritis and eczema. They are also vitally important in the retina of the eye and in the development of the brain.

Omega 3 fatty acids are found in all seafoods. Some also occur in some seeds and green vegetables, although the conversion of these to the same longer-chain omega 3 fats found in fish does not occur efficiently if the diet is too high in omega 6 fats.

Ideally, we should have some omega 6 fats and some omega 3 fats. Currently we have about 50 times as much of the omega 6s as the omega 3s. The ideal ratio is thought to be closer to 6 parts of omega 6s to one of omega 3s. In practice, this means eating less margarine and polyunsaturated vegetable oil and more fish. One to three fish meals a week is ideal. Some of this should be fresh fish; some can be canned.

Light & Easy Does It

FOR LUNCHES, WEEKEND MEALS or informal entertaining at any time, here are the recipes you'll turn to time and again. They're easy and quick to prepare, involving minimum effort for maximum return. When you're catering for all age groups, it can be hard to find dishes that are light enough for children and older folk, yet sufficiently satisfying for teenagers and adults. And, if there's a vegetarian in the house, this can be an additional consideration for the busy cook. You'll find all these options have been catered for. Try Vegetables with Peanut Sauce, Tuna Lasagne, Picnic Bread or Spinach and Salmon Roulade. These attractive meals are also ideal in hot weather when refreshing, light food is a must.

Picnic Bread (page 36) and Vegetables with Peanut Sauce (page 37)

Italian-style Sandwich

Full of flavour, this makes a simple and lovely lunch.

PREPARATION TIME: *20 minutes*
COOKING TIME: *10 minutes*
SERVES 6

*1 tablespoon virgin olive oil
1 large onion, sliced finely
4 baby eggplant (about 150g), sliced
1 red capsicum, seeded and sliced
2 teaspoons dried oregano leaves
12-15 black olives (about 60g)
1 piece focaccia (Italian flat bread),
about 250g*

1 Heat oil in a pan, add onion and cook with lid on over a gentle heat for 5 minutes.
2 Add eggplant and continue to cook, with lid on, for 10 minutes.
3 Add capsicum, oregano and olives and stir well to combine.
4 Split focaccia through centre. Pile filling on to bottom half, replace top of bread and bake on a flat foil-lined tray at 190°C for 10 minutes. Slice and serve immediately.

Nutritional information per serve:
Protein 6 g; fat 6 g; carbohydrate 26 g; good dietary fibre 3 g; sodium 485 mg; 780 kJ (185 Cals)

Other features: An excellent source of vitamin C and provides useful amounts of potassium

Italian Sandwich

Cornbread

Served with soup or salad, this is a good way to fill hungry people.

PREPARATION TIME: *15 minutes*
COOKING TIME: *25 minutes*
MAKES 16 *slices*

*1 cup plain wholemeal flour
1 tablespoon baking powder
1 cup cornmeal
1/2 cup wheatgerm
1 teaspoon dried thyme leaves
1 egg
1 1/4 cups skim milk*

*2 tablespoons grated Parmesan cheese
2 teaspoons paprika*

1 Sift flour and baking powder into a bowl. Tip bran remaining in sieve into bowl. Add cornmeal, wheatgerm and thyme.
2 Add egg, milk, 1 tablespoon of Parmesan and one teaspoon of paprika. Mix well and pour into a greased 18 cm square cake tin.
3 Mix remaining Parmesan and paprika and sprinkle over top of cornbread. Bake at 200°C for 25 minutes. Serve with a crisp salad.

Nutritional information per slice:
Protein 4 g; fat 2 g; carbohydrate 13 g; some dietary fibre 2 g; sodium 138 mg; 350 kJ (85 Cals)

Other features: Provides useful amounts of calcium

Picnic Bread

If you have never made bread, start by making this one. This recipe is delicious served for Sunday lunch or as part of a picnic spread.

PREPARATION TIME: *30 minutes + 1 hour while dough rises*
COOKING TIME: *40 minutes*
SERVES 8

*DOUGH
2 sachets dried yeast
1/2 cup warm water
1 teaspoon sugar
1 1/2 cups warm water
3 1/2 cups wholemeal flour
1 teaspoon chopped rosemary*

*FILLING
200 g cottage cheese
1/2 cup chopped basil
2 tablespoons toasted pine nuts
10 black olives, seeds removed
2 medium tomatoes (200 g), sliced
75 g thinly sliced low-fat Cheddar cheese
(7 per cent fat)
1 teaspoon olive oil
1 teaspoon chopped rosemary*

1 In a large bowl, combine yeast, 1/2 cup warm water and sugar. Leave for 10

minutes. Yeast mixture will be frothy.

2 Add remaining water, about 3¼ cups of the flour and the rosemary. Knead until well combined, using remaining flour if needed. Place ball of dough in a basin, cover with a plastic bag and leave to stand in a warm place until doubled in bulk (about 1 hour).

3 Punch dough down, cut into 2 pieces and roll each to a circle. Place one piece of dough on a greased oven tray and leave to stand for 10 minutes.

4 Spread cottage cheese over dough. Sprinkle with basil, pine nuts and olives. Arrange tomatoes and cheese on top.

5 Place second piece of bread dough on top and seal edges by pressing gently together.

6 Warm oil (a microwave makes this easy) and brush over surface of dough. Sprinkle with rosemary. Bake at 200°C for 40 minutes. Serve warm, cut into wedges.

Nutritional information per serve:
Protein 16 g; fat 5 g; carbohydrate 33 g; very good dietary fibre 6 g; sodium 185 mg; 1000 kJ (240 Cals)

Other features: A good source of thiamin, riboflavin, niacin and iron. Provides useful amounts of calcium and potassium

Vegetables with Peanut Sauce

This dish takes a little time to prepare and has a little more fat but it is a complete meal in itself.

PREPARATION TIME: *50 minutes*
COOKING TIME: *Nil*
SERVES 6

2 large potatoes, peeled
2 medium carrots, cut into thin strips
2 cups broccoli pieces
400 g green beans, trimmed
1 red capsicum, seeded and sliced
1 green capsicum, seeded and sliced
1 cucumber
1 cup mung-bean sprouts

SAUCE
2 tablespoons chicken stock
1 medium onion, chopped finely
2 cloves garlic, crushed

1 tablespoon tamarind purée (see Note)
50 g crushed peanuts
1 tablespoon salt-reduced soy sauce
1 tablespoon lemon juice
1 tablespoon crunchy peanut butter, no added salt
1 teaspoon chopped ginger
1 teaspoon chopped chilli
½ cup coconut milk

1 To make the sauce, heat chicken stock and gently cook onion and garlic for 3-4 minutes. Add remaining ingredients, bring to the boil, cover and simmer for 20 minutes, stirring occasionally and adding a little water if necessary to produce a thick sauce. While sauce is cooking, prepare vegetables.

2 Steam or microwave potatoes until tender. Cut into thick slices. Place in the centre of a large platter.

3 Individually steam or microwave carrots, broccoli and beans until barely tender. Immediately place in colander and run cold water over vegetables so they remain crisp. Drain and arrange on platter.

4 Arrange remaining vegetables on platter. Pour sauce over vegetables.

Note Tamarind purée is available at Asian food stores.

Nutritional information per serve:
Protein 11 g; fat 11 g; carbohydrate 19 g; excellent dietary fibre 8 g; sodium 140 mg; 900kJ (215 Cals)

Other features: Excellent source of vitamin C, potassium and vitamin A; very good source of niacin (B$_3$); good source of riboflavin, iron and zinc. Has some calcium content

The coconut 'milk' from the middle of a coconut has almost no fat and only 200 kJ (48 Cals) in 200 mL. Canned coconut milk comes from the coconut flesh and 200 mL has 1650 kJ (395 Cals).

Vegetables with Peanut Sauce

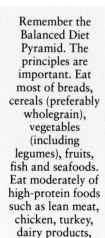

Tuna Lasagne

This is a fast and easy lasagne – great for those times when you have to entertain unexpected guests.

PREPARATION TIME: *20 minutes*
COOKING TIME: *30 minutes*
SERVES 6

½ cup sliced spring onions
1 clove garlic, crushed
2 cups chopped tomatoes, fresh or canned
1 tablespoon tomato paste, no added salt
2 tablespoons chopped parsley
freshly ground pepper
425 g tuna, no added salt
2 cups skim milk
2 tablespoons plain flour
2 eggs, beaten
pinch nutmeg
12 sheets instant lasagne
1 tablespoon grated Parmesan cheese
½ cup grated low-fat cheese,
½ teaspoon paprika

1 Combine the spring onions, garlic, tomatoes, tomato paste, parsley and pepper to taste. Gently mix in tuna.
2 Blend milk and flour and cook over a low heat until thick, or microwave, stirring often, on High for 3-4 minutes, until thick. Stir in beaten eggs and nutmeg.
3 Grease a casserole dish, dip lasagne noodles in hot water and spread 4 sheets over base of casserole. Top with half the tuna mixture. Repeat these layers and top with remaining lasagne noodles. Pour sauce over top. Sprinkle with combined cheeses and paprika and bake at 180°C for 30 minutes.

Nutritional information per serve:
Protein 28 g; fat 5 g; carbohydrate 28 g; good dietary fibre 3 g; sodium 400 mg; 1090 kJ (260 Cals)

Other features: An excellent source of niacin and a very good source of riboflavin. Also a good source of calcium, potassium, thiamin, iron and zinc and provides useful amounts of vitamins A, C and E

Risotto

Arborio rice is a short-grain product which can absorb large quantities of liquid to produce the creamiest-tasting rice. It is available from good delicatessens. This dish is wonderful with char-grilled chicken livers or with grilled chicken legs.

PREPARATION TIME: *10 minutes*
COOKING TIME: *35 minutes*
SERVES 6

1 tablespoon olive oil
1 medium-large onion, chopped
1¼ cups (250 g) Arborio rice (see Note)
4 bay leaves
sprig rosemary
7 or 8 saffron threads
4 cups hot chicken stock
½ cup white wine
1 cup peas
2 tablespoons almonds, chopped roughly
1 tablespoon grated Parmesan cheese
¼ cup sun-dried tomatoes

1 Heat oil and gently cook onion, without browning, for 3-4 minutes. Add rice and stir for 1-2 minutes. Add bay leaves and rosemary.
2 Add saffron to chicken stock and pour about 1 cup of stock into rice. Simmer uncovered until liquid is absorbed, then add another cup of stock. Repeat with a third cup of stock.
3 Add wine and peas and remaining stock. Continue cooking until all liquid is absorbed.
4 Add almonds, cheese and tomatoes and fold in gently with a fork. Cover and leave for about 3 minutes. Remove bay leaves and rosemary before serving.
Note If Arborio rice is unavailable, use a short-grain rice and reduce chicken stock to 3 cups.

Nutritional information per serve:
Protein 8 g; fat 7 g; carbohydrate 44 g; very good dietary fibre 5 g; sodium 175 mg; 1175 kJ (280 Cals)

Other features: Provides useful amounts of potassium and some vitamin C, niacin, thiamin, and iron

Remember the Balanced Diet Pyramid. The principles are important. Eat most of breads, cereals (preferably wholegrain), vegetables (including legumes), fruits, fish and seafoods. Eat moderately of high-protein foods such as lean meat, chicken, turkey, dairy products, eggs, nut or seeds. Eat least of fat and sugar.

Back: Risotto. Front: Tuna Lasagne

Cheese and Sage Damper

This damper is great in summer with salad or in winter with a bowl of piping hot soup. For the finest flavour, eat damper while still warm.

PREPARATION TIME: *10 minutes*
COOKING TIME: *30 minutes*
SERVES 8

90 g low-fat Cheddar cheese
2 cups wholemeal self-raising flour
½ teaspoon paprika
¼ teaspoon black pepper
1 teaspoon dried sage leaves
40 g low-fat/low-salt butter or margarine
1 cup evaporated skim milk
3 teaspoons milk
2 teaspoons grated Parmesan cheese
2 teaspoons poppy seeds

1 Using food processor, grate cheese. Mix in flour, paprika, pepper and sage.
2 Add butter or margarine and process until crumbly. Add evaporated milk and mix to a soft dough.
3 On a lightly floured surface, knead dough and shape into a 20 cm round. Using a sharp knife, cut almost through the dough into 8 wedges. Brush top with milk and sprinkle with Parmesan and poppy seeds. Bake at 180°C for 25-30 minutes. When slightly cooled, cut into wedges to serve.

Nutritional information per serve:
Protein 11 g; fat 4 g; carbohydrate 22 g; good dietary fibre 3 g; sodium 395 mg; 735 kJ (175 Cals)

Other features: A good source of calcium, thiamin and riboflavin and provides some iron, zinc and niacin

Pumpkin and Spinach Lasagne

This dish is popular with all age groups. It can be made and reheated in a microwave oven, or prepared up to the final stage and baked when ready to eat.

PREPARATION TIME: 40 *minutes*
COOKING TIME: *30 minutes*
SERVES 6

500 g pumpkin, peeled and sliced
1 bunch spinach
500 g ricotta cheese
½ cup sliced spring onions
½ cup chopped parsley
12 instant lasagne sheets
2 cups skim milk
2 tablespoons plain flour
2 eggs
¼ teaspoon nutmeg
1 cup grated Cheddar cheese, preferably low-fat

1 Steam pumpkin and spinach for 3 minutes each (or microwave spinach on High for 3 minutes and pumpkin on High for 2 minutes).
2 Combine spinach, ricotta, onions and parsley.
3 Dip lasagne sheets in hot water to soften slightly and arrange 3 sheets in a greased casserole. Top with a third of the pumpkin slices and a third of the spinach/ricotta mixture. Repeat twice. Top with remaining lasagne sheets.
4 Beat together milk, flour and eggs. Cook, stirring constantly until thick. Pour over lasagne, sprinkle with cheese and bake in a moderate oven for 30 minutes.

Nutritional information per serve:
Protein 25 g; fat 8 g; (or 14 g if regular cheese is used); carbohydrate 32 g; very good dietary fibre 7g (4g if white lasagne is used); sodium 386 mg; 1220 kJ (290 Cals) or 1435 kJ (340 Cals) if regular Cheddar cheese is used

Other features: Excellent source of vitamins A and C, very good source of potassium, good source of thiamin, riboflavin, zinc and iron. Rich in calcium

Vegetarian Fettuccine

PREPARATION TIME: *15 minutes*
COOKING TIME: *30 minutes*
SERVES 4

2 teaspoons olive oil
1 medium onion, sliced

Salt by another name: rock salt, sea salt, vegetable salt or 'natural' salt are all sodium chloride and have no health advantages over common salt. A bowl of cornflakes may contain more salt than a packet of potato crisps.

1 clove garlic, crushed
1 teaspoon mixed Italian herbs
1 medium eggplant, diced
500 g tomatoes, chopped
2 cups sliced mushrooms
1 capsicum, seeded and sliced
1 cup red wine
350 g fettuccine
2 tablespoons fresh chopped basil
2 tablespoons chopped parsley
1 tablespoon toasted pine nuts

1 In a large non-stick saucepan, heat oil, add onion, garlic and herbs, cover and cook over a gentle heat for 3-4 minutes.
2 Add eggplant, cover and cook for 2-3 minutes more.
3 Add tomatoes, mushrooms, capsicum and wine, bring to the boil, cover and simmer for 10 minutes. Remove lid and cook until thick.
4 Cook fettuccine in large pan of boiling water until just tender.
5 Add basil, parsley and pine nuts and serve over drained pasta.

Nutritional information per serve:
Protein 15 g; fat 6g carbohydrate 75 g; excellent dietary fibre 10 g; 1675 kJ (400 Cals)

Other features: An excellent source of vitamin C, a good source of the B-complex vitamins, vitamin A, potassium and iron and a useful source of zinc. Low sodium content (20 mg)

Vegetarian Fettuccine served with olives and Cheese and Sage Damper

Spinach and Salmon Roulade

This dish can be served warm or cold. Leftovers are great for the next day's lunch. Do not use silverbeet as its flavour is too coarse for this delicate dish.

PREPARATION TIME: *20 minutes*
COOKING TIME: *20 minutes*
SERVES 6

500 g spinach
¼ cup plain flour
2 tablespoons skim-milk powder
¼ cup chopped spring onions
3 eggs, separated
1 tablespoon wheatgerm
100 g sliced mushrooms
250 g cottage cheese
220 g can red salmon, drained
1 tablespoon chopped fresh lemon thyme
1 teaspoon finely grated lemon rind
freshly ground black pepper

Brie and Camembert cheese taste creamy but they have less fat than Cheddar. Cheddar has about 33 per cent fat; Brie has 29 per cent and Camembert averages 26 per cent. Low-fat Cheddar can go as low as 7 per cent fat.

1 Line a Swiss-roll tin with baking paper.
2 Steam or microwave shredded spinach. Purée spinach and add flour, milk powder, spring onions and egg yolks.
3 Beat egg whites until stiff and gently fold through spinach mixture. Pour into prepared tin and sprinkle with wheatgerm. Bake at 180°C for 20 minutes.
4 While roulade is baking, place mushrooms in a non-stick pan. Cook gently for 3-4 minutes.
5 Beat together cottage cheese, salmon, thyme, rind, pepper and mushrooms.
6 Turn roulade on to another piece of non-stick or greased baking paper. Gently spread filling over roulade and roll it up, using paper to help. Allow to stand for 5 minutes and serve warm. Or refrigerate and serve cold.

Nutritional information per serve:
Protein 20 g; fat 6 g; carbohydrate 6 g; good dietary fibre 3 g; sodium 285 mg; 665 kJ (155 Cals)

Other features: An excellent source of vitamin A, a good source of riboflavin, vitamin C, calcium, potassium and niacin. Also supplies iron and folic acid

1 *Carefully fold beaten egg whites into spinach mixture using a metal spoon.*

2 *Pour mixture evenly into greased and lined tin, sprinkle wheatgerm evenly over top.*

3 *Roll filled roulade from the short side, using the paper to help roll evenly.*

Chive and Pumpkin Soufflé

Serve this wonderful soufflé with a salad and some crusty wholemeal bread.

PREPARATION TIME: *20 minutes*
COOKING TIME: *15 minutes*
SERVES 4

3 tablespoons plain flour
1 cup skim milk
2 egg yolks
1 cup mashed pumpkin
1 tablespoon Dijon mustard
1 tablespoon chopped chives
3 egg whites

1 In a saucepan, make a paste with the flour and a little of the milk. Gradually add the remaining milk. Cook over a low heat until thick, stirring constantly.
2 Add egg yolks to milk mixture, beating well after each one. Add pumpkin, mustard and chives.
3 Beat egg whites until stiff. Fold about a quarter of the egg whites into the pumpkin mixture, then gently fold in remaining egg whites. Pour into 4 x 1 cup capacity greased soufflé dishes and bake at 190°C for 15 minutes.

Nutritional information per serve:
Protein 8 g; fat 3 g; carbohydrate 14 g; some dietary fibre 2 g; 460 kJ (110 Cals)

Other features: An excellent source of vitamin A and a good source of vitamin C and potassium. Useful amounts of calcium. Low sodium (80 mg)

Spinach Pie

PREPARATION TIME: *20 minutes*
COOKING TIME: *30 minutes*
SERVES 8

1 teaspoon butter or margarine
3 tablespoons (40 g) wheatgerm
600 g spinach
400 g ricotta cheese
4 eggs
pinch nutmeg
½ cup chopped spring onions
2 tablespoons chopped mint

1 Use butter or margarine to grease base of a 20 cm non-stick cake tin. Sprinkle with 2 tablespoons of the wheatgerm and press down with back of spoon.
2 Steam or microwave spinach until just wilted (about 3-4 minutes). Drain and press out as much water as possible.
3 Beat together ricotta, eggs and nutmeg.
4 Add spring onions, mint and spinach. Mix well and press on top of wheatgerm. Sprinkle with remaining tablespoon of wheatgerm. Bake at 180°C for 35 minutes.

Nutritional information per serve:
Protein 18 g; fat 11 g; carbohydrate 5 g; very good dietary fibre 5 g; sodium 230 mg; 840 kJ (200 Cals)

Other features: An excellent source of vitamins A and C, a very good source of potassium and a good source of iron and zinc. Rich in calcium

Healthy Quiche

This dish goes close to a real quiche in flavour – for only a fraction of the fat.

PREPARATION TIME: *10 minutes*
COOKING TIME: *40 minutes*
SERVES 4

8 sheets filo pastry
1 cup diced, cooked turkey
½ cup grated low-fat cheese
1 tablespoon chopped chives
375 g can evaporated skim milk
2 eggs

1 Grease a 23 cm quiche dish and line with pastry sheets, folding the edges to form a loose rim.
2 Sprinkle turkey, cheese and chives over pastry.
3 Beat evaporated milk and eggs together and pour over turkey mixture. Bake at 180°C for 40 minutes.

Nutritional information per serve:
Protein 35 g; fat 6 g; carbohydrate 24 g; dietary fibre 1 g; sodium 386 mg; 1230 kJ (295 Cals)

Other features: An excellent source of riboflavin, a very good source of niacin. Also a good source of potassium.

The ideal way to get vitamins is from food. Contrary to the claims of some companies selling vitamins, our food supply has plenty of vitamins. Our fruits, vegetables, grains, breads and cereal products are excellent sources, while protein foods such as meat, poultry, fish and dairy products are also potent suppliers of essential vitamins and minerals. If you decide to take vitamins, they may do you some good: if you are deficient in the vitamin in the first place; if you are taking some drug which destroys some vitamins; and if you believe in them.

Top left: Mushroom Rice Pie. Top right: Healthy Quiche (page 43) and Carrot and Lentil Patties with Tomato Sauce

Mushroom Rice Pie

A delightful lunch dish which can be served hot or cold with a tossed salad.

PREPARATION TIME: *20 minutes*
COOKING TIME: *30 minutes*
SERVES 6

PIE CRUST
1½ tablespoons sesame seeds
1½ cups cooked brown rice (½ cup raw)
1 egg, beaten
1 teaspoon dried parsley flakes

FILLING
2 tablespoons chicken stock
1 medium onion, sliced
1 medium capsicum, seeded and sliced
250 g mushrooms, sliced
2 eggs
¾ cup evaporated skim milk
1 tablespoon grated Parmesan cheese
¼ teaspoon paprika

1 Toast sesame seeds in a dry frying pan over a moderate heat until golden brown.
2 Mix all pie-crust ingredients together and press firmly into a greased 20 cm pie dish.
3 Heat chicken stock, add onion, cover and cook for 2-3 minutes. Add capsicum and mushrooms and cook without lid for a further 2-3 minutes, mixing gently. Spoon mushroom mixture into rice crust.
4 Beat eggs and milk and pour over mushrooms. Sprinkle with cheese and paprika and bake at 180°C for 30 minutes.

Nutritional information per serve:
Protein 16 g; fat 8 g; carbohydrate 27 g; good dietary fibre 4 g; sodium 180 mg; 995 kJ (235 Cals)

Other features: An excellent source of vitamin C and a good source of calcium, potassium, thiamin and niacin

Carrot and Lentil Patties with Tomato Sauce

These patties are wonderful hot but you'll also like them cold in pita bread with some alfalfa sprouts and shredded lettuce.

PREPARATION TIME: *5 minutes*
COOKING TIME: *35 minutes*
SERVES 6

1 cup red lentils
2 bay leaves
2 cups chicken stock
6 medium carrots
1 tablespoon chopped chives
2 tablespoons chopped almonds
1 egg
2 slices wholemeal bread, made into crumbs

SAUCE
425 g can tomatoes, chopped roughly
1 teaspoon dried oregano leaves
1 clove garlic, crushed
¼ cup red wine

1 Add lentils and bay leaves to chicken stock, bring to the boil, cover and cook over a low heat for 20 minutes. Discard bay leaves.
2 While lentils are cooking, grate carrots and mix with chives, almonds, egg and breadcrumbs.
3 To make sauce, place all ingredients in saucepan, bring to the boil and simmer, uncovered, for 5 minutes. Stir mixture occasionally.
4 Add lentils to carrot mixture and form into 6 patties.
5 Cook patties on a non-stick pan for 3-4 minutes on each side. Serve with sauce.

Nutritional information per serve:
Protein 13 g; fat 4 g; carbohydrate 28 g; excellent dietary fibre 8 g; sodium 150 mg; 840 kJ (200 Cals)

Other features: An excellent source of vitamin A. Also a very good source of iron, B-complex vitamins, potassium and vitamin C

Margarine has as many kilojoules as butter – both have a massive 615 kJ (145 Cals) in a tablespoon. Low-fat butters and margarines have about half this level. Low-fat margarines and low-fat butter cannot be used for frying as they contain either gelatine or maltodextrin – both will cause the food to stick firmly to the frying pan.

If your diet lacks vitamins, why not improve the diet? If you are tired, it is likely to be due to a lack of sleep, a deficiency of iron or a lack of sufficient food spread through the day. Vitamins are unlikely to help. There are only 8 genuine members of the vitamin B complex. These are thiamin (B_1), riboflavin (B_2), niacin (B_3), pantothenic acid (B_5), pyridoxine (B_6), folate, biotin and cyanocobalamin (B_{12}).

Vegetable Crumble

This dish can change to fit the seasons and is an ideal way to use up small quantities of different vegetables.

PREPARATION TIME: *10 minutes*
COOKING TIME: *30 minutes*
SERVES 6

2 teaspoons olive oil
1 medium onion, sliced
1 clove garlic
6 cups diced mixed vegetables (broccoli,
cauliflower, zucchini, carrot, asparagus,
whole button mushrooms, green beans)
425 g can tomatoes, roughly chopped

TOPPING
1 cup rolled oats
1 tablespoon butter or margarine
1 slice wholemeal bread, made
into crumbs
1 tablespoon toasted sunflower seeds
1 teaspoon dried basil leaves
1/2 cup grated low-fat cheese

1 Heat oil, add onion and garlic, cover and cook over a gentle heat for 3-4 minutes.
2 Add vegetables and tomatoes. Bring to the boil, simmer 3-4 minutes. Pour into 6 x 1 cup capacity ovenproof, individual casserole dishes.
3 Combine all ingredients for crumble topping and sprinkle over vegetables. Bake at 180°C for 20 minutes until golden.

Nutritional information per serve:
Protein 14 g; fat 11 g; carbohydrate 26 g; excellent dietary fibre 8 g; sodium 175 mg; 1110 kJ (265 Cals)

Other features: An excellent source of vitamins A and C, a good source of iron, zinc, calcium, potassium and the B-complex vitamins

Stuffed Capsicums

You can substitute hollowed-out tomatoes for the capsicums in this recipe. Either way, they are delicious served hot or taken cold as a picnic food.

PREPARATION TIME: *20 minutes*

COOKING TIME: *30 minutes (or 10-12 minutes in a microwave)*
SERVES 4

4 capsicums, red or green, preferably
'squat' shaped that stand upright
1/3 cup burghul
2/3 cup boiling water
2 teaspoons olive oil
1 medium onion, chopped finely
2 cups sliced mushrooms
2 tablespoons chopped mint
1/2 cup sliced celery
4 small cubes of low-fat Cheddar cheese

1 Cut a 'lid' from capsicums and carefully remove seeds.
2 Pour boiling water over burghul, cover tightly and leave to stand for 10 minutes (the water will be absorbed).
3 Heat olive oil, add onion, cover and leave to sweat for 5 minutes, stirring once or twice. Add mushrooms and cook a further 3-4 minutes.
4 Add mushroom mixture, mint and celery to burghul. Pile into capsicums and place in a small casserole so that capsicums stay upright.
5 Push a cube of cheese into the centre of each capsicum, replace 'lids' and bake at 180°C for 30 minutes, or microwave on High for 10-15 minutes.

Nutritional information per serve:
Protein 9 g; fat 4 g (or 8 g if regular Cheddar used); carbohydrate 15 g; good dietary fibre 4 g; 690 kJ (165 Cals) or 545 kJ (130 Cals) if low-fat cheese is used

Other features: Excellent source of vitamin C, a good source of potassium. Also a useful source of calcium, niacin and iron. Low sodium (120 mg)

Creamy Salmon Pasta

A fast, delicious meal. Tastes so creamy, but without any cream!

PREPARATION TIME: *15 minutes*
COOKING TIME: *20 minutes*
SERVES 4

250 g spiral or shell noodles or fettuccine
1/2 cup chicken stock
1/2 cup sliced spring onions

2 cups sliced mushrooms
1 red capsicum, seeded and sliced
1/2 cup chopped fresh basil
220 g can salmon, drained
1 cup evaporated skim milk
1 tablespoon grated Parmesan cheese
freshly ground black pepper

1 Cook pasta in a large pan of boiling water until just tender.
2 While pasta is cooking, heat chicken stock and add spring onions, mushrooms and capsicum. Cook 2 minutes, tossing ingredients gently.
3 Add basil, salmon, milk, cheese and pepper to mushroom mixture.
4 Drain pasta and add to the salmon sauce. Serve at once. accompanied by a tossed green salad.

Nutritional information per serve:
Protein 28 g; fat 6 g; carbohydrate 58 g; very good dietary fibre 6 g; sodium 445 mg; 1635 kJ (390 Cals)

Other features: An excellent source of vitamin C, a very good source of niacin, riboflavin and a good source of iron, zinc, vitamin A, potassium and thiamin. A rich source of calcium

Vegetable Crumble

ALL ABOUT CALCIUM

The body needs a constant level of calcium in the blood for the normal action of nerves and muscles. A hormone released from the parathyroid gland controls this level by balancing calcium from the diet with stores in bones. If there is not enough in the diet, the parathyroid hormone stimulates the release of calcium from the bones. If there is more calcium than is needed to keep the blood level constant, the excess can be deposited in bones. Greater withdrawals than deposits result in the bones gradually becoming less and less dense until they are so chalky that they fracture from a slight fall, or just with the effort of standing. The loss of calcium happens so slowly that it is many years before weakness and chalkiness eventuate. There are no symptoms before the final straw causes a fracture to occur.

A number of factors govern calcium absorption into bones. The positive factors which are essential for its occurrence include:
- calcium in the daily diet
- normal levels of hormones (these are vital for calcium to be retained by bones)
- weight-bearing exercise (calcium goes into bones when muscles exert a pull on the bone during physical activity)
- vitamin D (usually from sunlight on skin).

Some factors also work against calcium retention. These include:
- too much salt (increases loss of calcium in urine)
- too much protein (reduces retention of calcium)
- nicotine from cigarette and cigar smoking
- very high levels of caffeine or alcohol (small quantities are not a problem).

The chemical form of calcium may also be important. For example, we know that the type of calcium in milk and in dairy products is well absorbed. We do not yet know if the calcium in products such as soy milks is absorbed to the same extent.

Small, lightweight women have a lack of body weight and always have less pull of muscle on bone with weight-bearing exercise. They are more prone to weak, porous bones.

Blood tests are of little use in determining calcium levels in bone, because, as we have discussed, the body keeps its levels of blood calcium normal by withdrawing calcium from the bone. Blood tests are normal, therefore, even when bones are dangerously thin. A special type of X-ray machine is needed to measure bone density. Such tests are expensive but are recommended for women with a family history of fragile bones or spinal or hip problems.

Osteoporosis

The condition of porous bones is called osteoporosis. It is very common in older women and is related to the fall in oestrogen levels that accompanies menopause as well as a low-calcium diet, a lack of weight-bearing exercise and smoking. At the turn of this century, life expectancy for women was about 50 years, so few women lived long enough to develop osteoporosis. Over the past 20 or 30 years, many women have stopped working hard physically, no longer make a daily walk to the shops and carry home their food supplies and have less calcium in their daily diet.

Among Western women, one in five can expect to be hospitalised for a severe fracture to the hip or spine between the ages of 50 and 70. This is a great expense for the community and an enormous burden for the many women who must endure the pain of such calamities. As many as 40 per cent of all women can also expect to fracture wrists, ankles and other bones as a result of a slight fall at some stage in their life. Osteoporosis is also the reason why many older people become stooped, have back problems and appear to 'shrink' with age. 'Dowager's hump' is often the first sign of osteoporosis.

General recommendations for calcium intake

Age group	Calcium (mg)
Infants, 0-6 months,	
breast fed	300
bottle fed	500
Infants, 7-12 months	550
Children,	
1-3 years	700
4-7 years	800
Boys,	
8-11 years	800
12-15 years	1200
16-18 years	1000
Girls,	
8-11 years	900
12-15 years	1000
16-18 years	800
Men, all ages	800
Women,	
up to menopause	800
after menopause	1000
during pregnancy	1100
during lactation	1200

How hormones control calcium in bones

In growing children, growth hormone ensures that calcium is deposited into bones. In adults, the sex hormones take over this role. At menopause, when the oestrogen levels fall, calcium is no longer retained by the body. This may also occur in younger women and in female athletes if they lose so much body fat that their hormone levels change and their periods stop.

Osteoporosis also occurs in men, although the much slower loss of hormones and shorter life expectancy make it more rare.

Women at greatest risk of osteoporosis are those who:

- have had a low calcium intake throughout life
- are small and/or light
- have had little weight-bearing exercise.

To maintain bone density in women, most experts now recommend that those at risk of osteoporosis ask their doctor for hormone replacement therapy (HRT). This will cause their periods to continue past the usual menopause age but as they will be slight and regular, many women find it is worth the inconvenience to maintain their bone density.

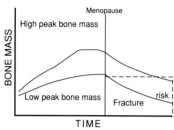

Importance of bone density

Types of bone

There are two types of bone to consider in osteoporosis. Cortical bone in the long bones of the arms and legs is lost when there is insufficient calcium in the blood and the parathyroid hormone causes it to be withdrawn from bone. Cortical bone is also lost if we are lacking in vitamin D (from the sun). Trabecular bone is spongy bone which is found in areas such as the spine. It is lost when hormone levels change and when the diet contains too much salt. Over a lifetime, women lose half their trabecular bone and one third of their cortical bone.

Too thin? Too much exercise?

Dieting disturbs the hormone balance. Losing body fat often causes periods to stop. When this occurs, trabecular bone from the spine is lost. Strenuous exercise can have the same effect.

This does not mean that women should stay fat and not exercise. Sensible, moderate dieting and increased exercise have a positive effect on health.

Girls and women with anorexia nervosa lose substantial amounts of bone and are at high risk of crushed vertebrae and other spinal problems and fractures. There is no evidence that a change to a better diet can undo the damage caused by periods of such intense dieting.

How much calcium?

The amount of calcium recommended for women varies. In Australia, recommended dietary intake is 800 mg per day. In some other countries, levels of 1200-1500 mg are recommended.

Many people think calcium is only important while children are growing. However, calcium continues to be absorbed into bones and peak bone density is not achieved until age 30-35 years. Women have so many bone problems after menopause that all young women and teenage girls should make sure they have plenty of calcium, some weight-bearing exercise and normal hormonal levels. Women should not become so thin that their periods stop.

We are genetically programmed so that different levels of body fat are appropriate for particular bodies. Any women who is so thin that her periods stop has reduced her body-fat to a level too low for her particular body. She may be fatter than someone else, but if her hormones are no longer functioning, she is too thin.

Sources of calcium

Dairy products contribute about 75 per cent of the calcium in most Western diets. In some Asian countries, calcium comes from small dried or fermented fish and from prawn shells which are eaten with the prawns or dried and powdered and used to give flavour to many other foods. Vegetables, soy beans, nuts, green vegetables and oranges also contribute some calcium.

Certain people do not digest dairy products well and for them they are unsuitable foods. But for most people of Anglo-Saxon background, dairy products are well-tolerated and represent the easiest way to get calcium.

Sesame seeds have been recommended as preferable to dairy products. However, they do not contain much calcium (see table) and it would be difficult to chew your way through the quantities needed to provide significant amounts of it. Some calcium values quoted for sesame seeds include the calcium present in the husks. Even if you could munch thoroughly enough for this calcium to be made available, the husks contain oxalic acid which forms a chemical complex with the calcium, tying it up so we cannot use it. Spinach also contains oxalic acid, so its calcium, too, is unavailable to the body. Making tahina is one way to grind enough sesame seeds to provide a richer source of calcium but as this paste is 50 per cent fat, it is not advisable to eat very much of it.

Food	Calcium content
Milk,	
regular or skim, 250 mL	290
low-fat (1 per cent fat), 250 mL	355
low-fat fortified, 250 mL	400
Buttermilk, 250 mL	300
Cheese, 30 g slice	230
Cottage cheese, 75 g	70
Ricotta cheese, 75 g	215
Yoghurt, low-fat, 200 g carton	390
Yoghurt, flavoured, 200 g carton	310
Salmon, canned, 100 g	310
Sardines, canned, 100 g	380
Crab, canned, drained, 100 g	155
Fresh fish, 200 g serve	75
Prawns, 6 medium	120
Oysters, 6	70
Almonds, 30 g	75
Baked beans, 140 g	65
Egg, 1	30
Sesame seeds, 1 teaspoon	5
Tahina, 1 tablespoon	35
Soy milk,	
regular, 250 mL	35
fortified, 250 mL	290
Broccoli, 100 g	30
Cabbage, 80 g	45
Orange, 1 medium	30

Main Attractions

MANY PEOPLE ARE UNDER THE IMPRESSION that 'healthy' eating is synonymous with 'boring' eating. If you have the idea that dreary grilled meat or baked fish without a vestige of a sauce are what constitute healthy food, think again. Imaginative, tasty food that isn't wicked and off-limits can be yours, as the recipes in this section prove. Stir-fried dishes, pasta and barbecued food can taste wonderful – and be very good for you. Cook Veal with Noodles, or Chicken with Prunes and Nuts for your family and you'll soon discover what healthy eating is really all about. If you love to entertain, try Barbecued Seafood. And, if children are proving hard to please, you won't go wrong with Bean Tacos, Seafood Pizza or Pasta with Chicken and Spring Vegetables. Adults love them, too.

Barbecued Seafood (page 52) and Pasta with Chicken and Spring Vegetables (page 52)

Pasta with Chicken and Spring Vegetables

Fettuccine, spiralli or penne shapes of pasta can be used for this recipe. Omit the chicken, if desired.

PREPARATION TIME: *5 minutes*
COOKING TIME: *25 minutes*
SERVES *4*

250 g pasta
3/4 cup chicken stock
1/2 cup sliced spring onions
1 bunch fresh asparagus, cut into 4cm pieces
1 cup snow peas, topped and tailed
1 cup shredded cooked chicken
3/4 cup ricotta cheese
1/2 cup low-fat yoghurt
2 tablespoons lemon juice
1 teaspoon prepared mild mustard
1/4 teaspoon dried chillies

1 Cook pasta in a large pan of boiling water until just tender. Drain.
2 While pasta is cooking, heat 1/4 cup of the chicken stock, add spring onions, asparagus and snow peas and simmer for 2 minutes. Add chicken and stir lightly.
3 Blend ricotta, yoghurt, lemon juice, mustard and remaining 1/2 cup of chicken stock. Add to vegetables, stir until boiling. Serve over hot pasta. Garnish with dried chillies.

Nutritional information per serve:
Protein 25 g; fat 6 g; carbohydrate 53 g; very good dietary fibre 6 g; sodium 143 mg; calcium 225 mg; 1540 kJ (370 Cals)

Other features: Good source of calcium, vitamin C, niacin and potassium and supplies some iron

Barbecued Seafood

Served with a tossed salad and some crusty bread, this meal is hard to beat. Octopus must be cooked on a very hot plate or pan. Do not overcook or they will be tough.

PREPARATION TIME: *20 minutes + 1 hour marinating time*

COOKING TIME: *5 minutes*
SERVES *4*

1/2 cup red wine
1 tablespoon olive oil
2 cloves garlic, crushed
2 tablespoons chopped parsley
8 baby octopus (remove heads and 'beaks' in centre of tentacles; cut tentacles in halves)
12 green king prawns
8 scallops
freshly ground pepper

1 Combine wine, oil, garlic and parsley and marinate octopus for an hour or more (in refrigerator).
2 Have barbecue plate very hot (if indoors, heat a large pan until very hot). Remove octopus from marinade, dry on paper towels and cook for 4-5 minutes.
3 Add prawns and cook for 3-4 minutes. Add scallops and cook for 1-2 minutes (they toughen if overcooked). Serve seafood immediately with ground pepper.

Nutritional information per serve:
Protein 31 g; fat 4 g; no carbohydrate; no dietary fibre; sodium 510 mg; 675 kJ (160 Cals)

Other features: An excellent source of iodine, a good source of potassium, niacin, thiamin, iron and zinc. Also provides useful amounts of calcium

Seafood Pizza

It does take time to make bread dough but it's fun and the taste of home-made pizza is well worth the effort.

PREPARATION TIME: *30 minutes + 1 hour standing time*
COOKING TIME: *20 minutes*
SERVES *6*

CRUST
1 tablespoon dried yeast
2 tablespoons lukewarm water
1 teaspoon sugar
3/4 cup wholemeal flour
3/4 cup plain flour
1/2 cup lukewarm water
1 teaspoon dried Italian herbs
2 teaspoons olive oil

Preservatives help control moulds, bacteria and other micro-organisms in foods. In the majority of cases, preservatives are much better than micro-organisms. Using modern preservatives may also allow greater retention of nutrients than traditional methods of salting and drying foods. No preservatives are needed in canned foods as the exclusion of oxygen and heat treatment kill micro-organisms. Preservatives are used in a wide range of foods and drinks. In some cases, they make valuable foods safer to eat.

FILLING
½ cup tomato paste (no added salt)
2 teaspoons dried oregano leaves
1 large onion, sliced
*250 g seafood marinara mix (small
prawns, scallops, mussels)*
*1 red capsicum, seeded and cut into
thin strips*
½ cup grated low-fat Cheddar cheese
2 tablespoons grated Parmesan cheese
12 black olives

1 Combine yeast, 2 tablespoons water
and sugar and leave for 10-15 minutes
until bubbles appear.
2 Sift flours. Add remaining water, herbs,
yeast mixture and oil and mix well. Knead
well until smooth and shiny, adding a little
more flour if necessary. Place in a greased
bowl, place bowl in a large plastic bag and
leave in a warm place until doubled in bulk
(for approximately 1 hour).
3 Punch dough down, knead well and roll
out to a 30 cm circle. Place on a greased
pizza tray.
4 Spread tomato paste over pizza dough.
Sprinkle with oregano, sliced onion,
seafood, capsicum and cheese and arrange
olives on top. Bake at 200°C for 20
minutes.

Nutritional information per serve:
Protein 20 g; fat 6 g; carbohydrate 24 g;
good dietary fibre 3 g; 985 kJ (230 Cals);
sodium 410 mg

Other features: An excellent source of
thiamin, a good source of calcium, potassium, iron, vitamin C and niacin

*Chicken Breast with
Flaming Sauce*

If you make the sauce ahead, this dish can
be ready minutes after you get home.

PREPARATION TIME: *15 minutes*
COOKING TIME: *12 minutes*
SERVES *4*

*4 chicken breast fillets
chives, for garnish*

SAUCE
*3 medium-sized tomatoes, very ripe
2 teaspoons olive oil*

*1 small onion, chopped roughly
1 clove garlic, crushed
1 tablespoon paprika
½ teaspoon dried thyme
1 large red capsicum, seeded and sliced*

*Chicken Breast with
Flaming Sauce*

1 Pour boiling water over tomatoes, leave
for 1 minute then plunge them into cold
water. Remove skins and dice roughly.
2 Heat oil and cook onion, covered, for
2-3 minutes. Add garlic, paprika and
thyme and cook a further 1 minute. Add
capsicum and tomatoes and cook for 10
minutes or until soft. Purée mixture until
smooth.
3 While sauce is cooking, grill or barbecue chicken breasts for 6-8 minutes,
turning once (do not overcook). Serve the
chicken breasts on top of sauce and
garnish each serve with a couple of
whole chives.

Nutritional information per serve:
Protein 30 g; fat 5 g; carbohydrate 5 g;
good dietary fibre 3 g; 800 kJ (190 Cals)

Other features: An excellent source of
niacin, a good source of potassium,
thiamin, riboflavin and vitamin C. Also
provides some iron, zinc and vitamin A.
Low sodium (75 mg)

Chicken and Oat Loaf with Red Capsicum Sauce; Beef, Beans and Beer Casserole (page 57)

 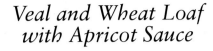

Chicken and Oat Loaf with Red Capsicum Sauce

This is delicious cold, served in pita bread with alfalfa and crisp lettuce.

PREPARATION TIME: *15 minutes*
COOKING TIME: *50 minutes*
SERVES 6

500 g minced chicken
1 cup rolled oats
1/4 cup evaporated skim milk
1 egg, beaten
1 cup grated carrot
1 cup chopped mushrooms
1/2 cup sliced spring onions
1 teaspoon dried rosemary
1/2 cup chopped parsley
2 tablespoons toasted sesame seeds

SAUCE
1 red capsicum, seeded and chopped roughly
3/4 cup chicken stock
freshly ground pepper

1 Combine all ingredients for the loaf except sesame seeds.
2 Grease a loaf tin and sprinkle 1 tablespoon sesame seeds over the base. Press chicken mixture into tin and sprinkle with remaining sesame seeds. Bake at 180°C for 45-50 minutes. Allow to stand 5 minutes before turning out. If serving loaf cold, allow to cool in tin.
3 To make the sauce, place capsicum and stock into a small saucepan, bring to the boil, cover and simmer for 6-7 minutes. Purée in blender, adding pepper to taste. Serve warm.

Nutritional information per serve:
Protein 26 g; fat 6 g; carbohydrate 16 g; good dietary fibre 3 g; 950 kJ (225 Cals)

Other features: Very good source of vitamin A, a good source of riboflavin, potassium and niacin. Some iron, calcium and zinc. Low sodium (110 mg)

Veal and Wheat Loaf with Apricot Sauce

This loaf is delicious hot or cold with salad or on sandwiches. The sweetness of the apricots makes it popular with children.

PREPARATION TIME: *30 minutes*
COOKING TIME: *65 minutes*
SERVES 6

1 cup burghul
1/2 cup chopped dried apricots
1 1/4 cups boiling water
1 medium onion, chopped finely
500g minced veal
1 teaspoon ground allspice
1/2 teaspoon coarsely ground black pepper
1 tablespoon chopped mint
2 teaspoons finely grated orange rind
1 tablespoon pine nuts

SAUCE
1/2 cup orange juice
1/2 cup chicken stock
1/4 cup dried apricots

1 Combine burghul and apricots in a bowl. Pour boiling water over, cover bowl tightly and then leave to stand for 15-20 minutes (water will be absorbed).
2 Add all ingredients to wheat, except pine nuts. Mix thoroughly and pack into a greased loaf tin. Press pine nuts into top of loaf. Bake in a moderate oven for 1 hour. Let stand 5 minutes before turning out. Serve hot with apricot sauce or cold with a spicy chutney.
3 To make the sauce, combine all ingredients in small saucepan, bring to the boil, cover and simmer for 15 minutes. Purée until smooth.

Nutritional information per serve (with sauce):
Protein 23 g; fat 3 g; carbohydrate 26 g; very good dietary fibre 7 g; 905 kJ (215 Cals)

Other features: A good source of potassium, iron, zinc and niacin. Low sodium (100 mg)

If you think a fat loss of 0.5 kg a week isn't much, imagine losing the equivalent amount of fat as in a tub of margarine! To convert kilojoules to Calories, divide by 4.2. 420 kJ equals 100 Cals.

Fish and Rice Balls

These steamed fish balls are great as a first course or served with stir-fried vegetables as a main course.

PREPARATION TIME: *30 minutes + 2 hours for soaking rice*
COOKING TIME: *15 minutes*
SERVES 6

1 cup rice
2 cups water
400 g boneless white fish fillets
1 small can water chestnuts, drained and chopped
½ cup sliced spring onions
1 cup chopped fresh coriander
1 teaspoon chopped fresh ginger
1 tablespoon fish sauce
2 egg whites

1 Soak rice in water for at least 2 hours. Drain and tip into a shallow bowl.
2 Place fish in a food processor and mince. Add remaining ingredients and mix well.
3 Using wet hands, take out a tablespoonful of the fish mixture and roll it in the rice. Continue in this way – mixture should make 16-18 balls.
4 Place the fish balls on lightly oiled greaseproof paper in a steamer (bamboo or stainless steel – or use a metal rack or tiny non-stick muffin pans on a rack in a frying pan). Place water in base of steamer, cover and steam fish balls for 15 minutes.

Nutritional information per fish ball:
Protein 6 g; fat less than 1 g; carbohydrate 9 g; dietary fibre 0.5 g; 270 kJ (65 Cals)

Other features: Provides some B-complex vitamins and iron. Has a low sodium content (70 mg)

Fish sauces are low in kilojoules but they vary considerably. Thai fish sauce has 15 kJ/tablespoon (3 Cals) whereas high quality nuoc-nam fish sauce from Vietnam may contain over 200 kJ/tablespoon (48 Cals). Tamarind is often used in Indian recipes. It is a fruit whose pods have a slightly sour flavour. It is high in dietary fibre. One teaspoon has 50 kJ (13 Cals).

1 *Using wet hands, roll tablespoonfuls of the fish mixture into evenly shaped balls.*

2 *Roll fish balls over drained rice to coat each evenly.*

3 *Place fish balls on lightly oiled paper in steamer.*

Beef, Beans and Beer Casserole

The alcohol from the beer evaporates during cooking but leaves a great yeasty flavour that enhances this dish.

PREPARATION TIME: *20 minutes*
COOKING TIME: *2 hours*
SERVES 6

500 g lean stewing steak, trimmed of all fat, cut into 2 cm cubes
1 large onion, cut into eighths
1 medium eggplant, diced
½ teaspoon dry mustard
1 teaspoon dried basil leaves
1 cup low-alcohol beer
425 g can red kidney beans

1 Using a non-stick pan, brown meat. Place in casserole dish.
2 In the same pan, brown onion. Place on top of meat.
3 Add eggplant, mustard, basil, beer and beans plus their liquid to meat. Stir well. Bake covered at 150°C for 2 hours, or until beef is very tender.

Nutritional information per serve:
Protein 29 g; fat 4 g; carbohydrate 12 g; excellent dietary fibre 8 g; sodium 145 mg; 860 kJ (205 Cals)

Other features: Good source of B-complex vitamins, iron, zinc and potassium

Lamb Fillets in Whisky Sauce

PREPARATION TIME: *30 minutes*
COOKING TIME: *6 minutes*
SERVES 4

2 tablespoons whisky
2 tablespoons mango chutney
8 lamb fillets (about 70 g each)
¾ cup evaporated skim milk
2 teaspoons cornflour
1 tablespoon water

1 Combine whisky and chutney in a shallow dish. Place lamb fillets in mixture, turn them to coat and leave for 30 minutes to marinate.
2 Remove lamb from marinade and place in a hot non-stick pan. Reserve marinade. Cook lamb for no more than 5-6 minutes, turning once.
3 While lamb is cooking, heat milk, add combined cornflour and water and the remaining marinade. Stir constantly until boiling. Serve with lamb.

Nutritional information per serve:
Protein 36 g; fat 5 g; carbohydrate 15 g; no dietary fibre; sodium 235 mg; 1050 kJ (250 Cals)

Other features: Good source of iron, zinc, niacin, calcium and potassium

Chicken with Prunes and Nuts

PREPARATION TIME: *5 minutes*
COOKING TIME: *25 minutes*
or 12 minutes in a microwave
SERVES 4

½ cup pitted prunes
2 tablespoons blanched almonds
½ cup dry sherry
¼ cup orange juice
1 teaspoon ground cinnamon
1 teaspoon finely grated orange rind
600 g chicken thigh fillets
freshly ground black pepper
1 tablespoon chopped fresh coriander

1 Place prunes, almonds, sherry, juice, cinnamon and orange rind in a saucepan and bring to the boil, or microwave on High for 2 minutes.
2 Add chicken and pepper, cover and simmer for 20 minutes, or microwave, covered, on High for 8-10 minutes, or until chicken is tender. Sprinkle with coriander. Serve with rice, cracked wheat or noodles.

Nutritional information per serve:
Protein 31 g; fat 9 g; carbohydrate 13 g; very good dietary fibre 5 g; 1070 kJ (255 Cals)

Other features: A very good source of riboflavin and niacin and a good source of potassium, zinc and iron. Low sodium (120 mg)

Moths have good taste – they always attack the most nutritious items – wholegrains, brown rice, nuts. Store nuts in the refrigerator to help prevent them going rancid. Keep wheatgerm in the refrigerator to preserve its vitamin E.

Barbecued Cod

This is an easy way to cook fish. A barbecue is ideal or use a griller lined with foil.

PREPARATION TIME: *5 minutes + 30 minutes for marinating*
COOKING TIME: *8-10 minutes*
SERVES 4

½ cup white wine
2 tablespoons lemon juice
1 teaspoon coarsely cracked pepper
2 tablespoons chopped fresh herbs (use thyme, parsley, rosemary, oregano or a mixture of any of these)
4 cod steaks, about 750 g (or any other white fish)

1 Combine wine, juice, pepper and herbs in a shallow dish. Place fish in mixture, turn each steak over and leave for at least 30 minutes (or cover and place in refrigerator all day).
2 Remove fish from marinade and place on a hot barbecue or under a pre-heated grill. Cook for no more than 8-10 minutes, turning once. When fish flakes easily it is cooked. Do not overcook.
3 While fish is cooking, heat remaining marinade and cook until reduced slightly. Pour over cooked fish.

Nutritional information per serve:
Protein 29 g; fat 6 g*; no carbohydrate; no dietary fibre; sodium 225 mg; 700 kJ (165 Cals)

Other features: A good source of iodine, potassium and the B-complex vitamins, provides some iron, calcium and zinc
* Fat content will vary with the fish used

Many people dislike fish because they overcook it. Most fish take only a few minutes for their flesh to become opaque and cooked. If fish flakes easily it is cooked. Look for canned tuna, salmon and sardines in a water pack. Saves fat compared with the oil-packed variety and salt compared with those that are packed in brine.

Veal with Noodles

An all-in-one dish which is great served in deep bowls. If fresh noodles are unavailable, use dried.

PREPARATION TIME: *10 minutes*
COOKING TIME: *20 minutes*
SERVES 4

250 g fresh egg noodles
2 teaspoons sesame oil
1 large onion, sliced
1 clove garlic, crushed
1 teaspoon chopped chilli
500 g veal steak, cut into strips
½ cup chicken stock
½ cup sliced spring onions
1 red capsicum, seeded and sliced
1 cup sliced broccoli
1 cup sliced green beans
½ cup chopped fresh coriander
2 teaspoons cornflour
2 tablespoons water

1 Drop noodles into a large saucepan of boiling water, cook until just tender (about 3 minutes) and drain well.
2 In a large non-stick wok or frying pan, heat oil and gently cook onion, garlic and chilli for 3-4 minutes. Remove onion.
3 Make sure pan is hot then add veal. Stir-fry for 3-4 minutes or until just beginning to brown. Add to onion.
4 Add chicken stock to pan, heat and stir in any 'bits' from pan. Add vegetables and coriander. Cover and simmer for 3-4 minutes.
5 Add veal, onions and noodles and stir until hot. Stir in combined cornflour and water, cook 1 minute and serve.

Nutritional information per serve:
Protein 39 g; fat 5 g; carbohydrate 41 g; very good dietary fibre 5 g; 1530 kJ (365 Cals)

Other features: A very good source of iron, vitamins A and C and the B-complex vitamins and a good source of potassium. Low sodium (100 mg)

Chicken with Prunes and Nuts (page 57)

Veal with Noodles and Barbecued Cod

Mustard Beef Kebabs

A few minutes preparation in the morning and it takes very little time to cook this dish when you get home from work.

PREPARATION TIME: *10 minutes + standing time*
COOKING TIME: *10 minutes*
SERVES *4*

2 tablespoons grainy mustard
1 teaspoon prepared horseradish
2 teaspoons brown sugar
2 tablespoons brandy (or orange juice)
1/2 cup low-fat yoghurt
500 g lean rump steak, cut into
2.5 cm cubes
2 medium onions, cut into wedges

1 Combine mustard, horseradish, sugar, brandy or juice and yoghurt. Toss beef in yoghurt mixture. Leave, covered, in the refrigerator for at least 30 minutes (or all day).
2 Thread meat and onion on to 8 skewers (soaked in water to prevent burning) and grill or barbecue for 5-10 minutes, brushing several times with yoghurt mixture. Serve with steamed new potatoes and a green vegetable or salad.

Nutritional information per serve:
Protein 32 g; fat 4 g; carbohydrate 6 g; dietary fibre 1 g; 820 kJ (195 Cals)

Other features: A very good source of zinc, niacin and riboflavin, a good source of potassium, thiamin and iron. Low sodium (95 mg)

When used in cooking, the alcohol in wines and spirits evaporates but leaves behind delicious flavours. You do not need to count the kilojoules from wines used in foods which have been boiled or heated.

Herbed Chicken

This dish is just as good on a hot summer night as it is in colder weather.

PREPARATION TIME: *10 minutes*
COOKING TIME: *35 minutes*
SERVES *4*

4 chicken breast fillets
2 teaspoons oil
2 medium onions, sliced
1/4 cup white vinegar
1/2 cup mint leaves

1/4 cup fresh coriander
1 clove garlic
1 teaspoon chopped ginger
1 teaspoon chopped chilli

1 Trim breasts of fat, make criss-cross cuts across one side of each fillet. Combine oil, onions, vinegar, mint, coriander, garlic, ginger and chilli in food processor, process until finely chopped.
2 Brush a little herb mixture evenly over each chicken breast, place under a medium hot grill, cook until just tender.
3 Serve chicken breasts with the remaining herb mixture and a salad.

Nutritional information per serve:
Protein 17 g; fat 7 g; carbohydrate 3 g; dietary fibre 1 g; 585 kJ (140 Cals)

Other features: A good source of niacin and riboflavin and provides some potassium, iron and zinc. Low sodium (70 mg)

Bean Tacos

One of the easiest meals to have on hand and always popular with teenagers. For smaller children, reduce or omit chilli. If you do not want a vegetarian meal, add 200 g of chopped turkey with the beans. If starting with raw kidney beans, soak and cook 1 cup of beans.

PREPARATION TIME: *15 minutes*
COOKING TIME: *20 minutes*
SERVES *4*

2 teaspoons olive oil
1 medium onion, chopped
1 teaspoon chopped fresh chilli (more or
less to taste)
1 clove garlic, crushed
2 1/2 cups cooked kidney beans
400 g can tomatoes, chopped roughly
250 g mushrooms, sliced
1 teaspoon dried thyme
1 tablespoon tomato paste (no
added salt)
taco shells

1 Heat oil in medium-sized saucepan, add onion, chilli and garlic, cover pan. Leave

onion mixture to sweat for 2-3 minutes.

2 Add remaining bean mixture ingredients, bring to the boil and simmer for 10 minutes.

3 Heat taco shells and serve with bean mixture, chopped fresh tomatoes, shredded lettuce and low-fat yoghurt.

Nutritional information per serve, bean mixture only:
Protein 14 g; fat less than 3 g; carbohydrate 24 g; excellent source of dietary fibre 14 g; 730 kJ (130 Cals)

Other features: A very good source of potassium, a good source of B-complex vitamins, iron, zinc and vitamin C. Low sodium (55 mg)

Green Curry

This simple dish fills the kitchen with wonderful aromas. It takes only a few minutes to make. Even non-vegetarians will love it.

PREPARATION TIME: *10 minutes*
COOKING TIME: *20 minutes*
SERVES *4*

1 tablespoon unsalted butter or oil
2 medium-large onions, each cut into quarters
1 teaspoon ground cumin
1 teaspoon ground fenugreek
1 tablespoon ground coriander
1 teaspoon chopped ginger
1 teaspoon chopped chilli
4 medium tomatoes, chopped roughly
400 g green beans, topped and tailed
250 g defrosted frozen spinach
3/4 cup water

1 Heat butter or oil and gently cook onion and spices for 4-5 minutes, stirring several times.

2 Add remaining ingredients, bring to the boil, cover, simmer, stirring occasionally, for 10-15 minutes. Serve with boiled rice and pappadams.

Nutritional information per serve:
Protein 6 g; fat 4 g; carbohydrate 8 g; excellent dietary fibre 9 g; 420 kJ (100 Cals)

Other features: An excellent source of vitamin C, a very good source of iron and potassium, a good source of vitamin A. Also provides useful amounts of calcium. Low sodium (30 mg)

Pork with Pears and Juniper Berries

Place juniper berries in a plastic bag and hit with a rolling pin to crush.

PREPARATION TIME: *25 minutes*
COOKING TIME: *15 minutes*
SERVES *4*

1 tablespoon honey
1 tablespoon salt-reduced soy sauce
2 tablespoons gin (or use orange juice)
600 g lean pork fillets
1½ tablespoons juniper berries, crushed
2 teaspoons olive oil
2 pears, peeled, cored and cut in halves
¼ teaspoon cinnamon

1 In a shallow dish, mix together honey, soy sauce and gin (or juice). Dip pork fillets into this mixture and then into juniper berries, pressing berries into pork.

2 Heat a non-stick pan, add oil and cook pork for 8-10 minutes, turning once.

3 While pork is cooking, slice each pear half without cutting right through (so slices can fan out). Push pork to one side of pan, add pears to pan, sprinkle with cinnamon and cook for a further 2-3 minutes until pears are hot but still firm. Serve with steamed vegetables and new potatoes.

Nutritional information per serve:
Protein 35 g; fat 5 g; carbohydrate 16 g; some dietary fibre 2 g; sodium 245 mg; 1030 kJ (245 Cals)

Other features: An excellent source of thiamin, a very good source of other B-complex vitamins and a good source of potassium, iron and zinc

Always make sure a pan or barbecue plate is hot before cooking meat. When hot, brush on a little oil and then add meat. A cold pan will absorb much more oil. A hot surface 'seals' the meat. Olive oil can be taken to a much higher temperature before the fats change their structure compared with other cooking oils.

Thai-style Fish

Put some rice on to cook, start preparing the fish and you can sit down to dinner within 30 minutes. Speed up the process by slicing mint and lemon grass together.

PREPARATION TIME: *15 minutes*
COOKING TIME: *15 minutes*
SERVES 4

1 teaspoon oil
4 spring onions, sliced
1 clove garlic, crushed
½ teaspoon chopped chilli
3 sprigs mint, sliced finely
3 stalks lemon grass, sliced finely
4 fish steaks or fillets
½ cup chopped fresh coriander
1 tablespoon lemon juice
1 teaspoon fish sauce
2 tomatoes, cut into eighths

1 Using a non-stick pan, heat oil, add spring onions, garlic, chilli, mint and lemon grass. Stir over a gentle heat for 2-3 minutes.
2 Add fish and cook for 5-7 minutes, turning once. Remove fish steaks and keep them warm.
3 Add remaining ingredients to pan and cook for 3-4 minutes (tomatoes should be hot but not mushy). Pour over fish steaks.

Nutritional information per serve:
Protein 32 g; fat 3 g; carbohydrate 4 g; no dietary fibre; sodium 280 mg; 750 kJ (180 Cals)

Other features: An excellent source of niacin, iodine, a very good source of potassium, a good source of vitamin C and provides some vitamin A and calcium

It is fine to drink water with meals as long as it is not used to 'wash down' unchewed food. Orange juice has no alcohol but it does have kilojoules. A glass of orange juice has more kilojoules than a glass of beer.

Pork Fillets with Mango Sauce

This is one of those wonderfully easy dishes that seems very special. If fresh mangoes are out of season, drained, canned mangoes can be used.

PREPARATION TIME: *15 minutes*
COOKING TIME: *10 minutes*
SERVES 4

flesh of 1 large mango
2 tablespoons mango chutney
2 teaspoons Dijon mustard
2 tablespoons port
2 tablespoons lemon juice
2 teaspoons oil
500 g pork fillet, sliced
1 medium onion, diced

1 In blender combine mango, chutney, mustard, port and lemon juice. Blend briefly so that the mixture retains some texture.
2 In a non-stick pan, heat oil and stir-fry pork fillet for 2-3 minutes. Add onion and continue stir-frying for a further 2-3 minutes.
3 Pour mango sauce over pork and heat until just boiling. Serve at once with noodles, steamed rice or steamed potatoes and vegetables or salad.

Nutritional information per serve:
Protein 23 g; fat 4 g; carbohydrate 9 g; dietary fibre 1 g; 695 kJ (165 Cals)

Other features: An excellent source of thiamin and niacin, a very good source of riboflavin and zinc and provides some iron, potassium, vitamin A and vitamin C. Low sodium (80 mg)

Thai-style Fish

Back: Mustard Beef Kebabs (page 60). Front: Pork Fillets with Mango Sauce

ALL ABOUT SALT

Once considered a simple substance, salt is now confusing many people. Do we need it? How much do we need? Is it harmful? Should we choose sea salt, rock salt, vegetable salt, natural salt, sun-dried salt, iodised salt, cooking salt, salt substitute or just plain common salt? Or should we buy items that claim to be unsalted, have no added salt or are salt-free?

Salt and sodium
Some people do become confused by these terms. Salt is sodium chloride; the sodium makes up about 40 per cent of the salt molecule. Sodium occurs naturally in almost all foods, even in those to which no salt has been added. When salt is added, the total sodium content increases. Added salt contributes far more sodium than the naturally occurring sodium.

If you are following a low salt diet (for example, those with high blood pressure), do not add salt in cooking or at the table and avoid processed foods with added salt. The sodium which occurs naturally is rarely a problem.

How much salt?
We all need the sodium and chloride found in salt. Along with potassium, sodium helps maintain the balance between water inside and around the cells, keeps blood volume normal and also controls the acidity balance in the body. Few people need to eat added salt since both sodium and chloride are found naturally in many foods. All seafoods are rich in these elements, as are meats, eggs and milk. Some vegetables are also adequate sources.

Most people eat too much salt and their kidneys must get rid of the excess sodium. This requires water and the thirst experienced after a particularly salty meal is designed to make us provide the kidneys with the extra water they need to excrete excess sodium from the salt. The kidneys also look after sodium balance at the other end of the scale. If we take in too little sodium, the kidneys will conserve it very efficiently.

Babies have great difficulty excreting salt and even a formula milk that is made up too strongly will contain so much sodium that it puts an enormous strain on their immature kidneys. Babies do not inherently like salt and turn up their noses at their first salted foods. However, most adults keep giving salted foods to children and their taste-buds become used to the flavour.

Eating heavily salted foods is also a cause of stomach cancer — this is the most common form of cancer in the world. Stomach cancer has decreased dramatically in Western countries since people began to preserve food with refrigeration and freezing instead of by salting.

Salt and blood pressure
The kidneys do a good job of getting rid of excess sodium but after years of effort they can fall down on the task and start to retain it. The extra water in the blood then causes small blood vessels to become overly sensitive to signals which cause them to contract. The heart must then work harder to force blood through these narrow stiffened blood vessels and blood pressure rises. Not everyone is equally sensitive to the effects of excess sodium, but since we cannot yet predict who will become salt-sensitive, it makes sense for everyone to cut back on salt.

Daily needs for sodium
Adults should aim for a sodium intake between 1000 and 2300 mg a day. Since about 40 per cent of salt is sodium, this equates to about 2.5-6 grams of salt a day. Children under 12 years of age should eat a little less than this. One to three year-olds should be having 300-1200 mg of sodium and those under 12 months 140-280 mg a day. Babies under 12 months should not have salt added to their foods. A slice of bread with a thin spread of yeast extract could fit into an infant's diet, as long as salty breakfast cereals and other salted foods were not a regular part of the diet. Prepared baby foods have no added salt. It is best for everyone to avoid salt in cooking and at the table and to choose unsalted processed foods where possible. However, there is no need for most people to go to extremes of avoiding bread or yeast extract or even the occasional anchovy.

Taste
Once our taste-buds become used to the flavour of salt, the liking for it tends to stay. If you decide to reduce the salt in your diet, you need to allow about three months for your taste-buds to adjust and gradually learn to like the natural flavour of unsalted foods. Salt certainly adds flavour to foods - it adds the flavour of salt.

Try microwaving vegetables without water, steaming them or stir-frying them briefly either in concentrated chicken stock or in a little oil. You will find they retain so much of their original flavour that salt becomes obsolete.

When making stews or casseroles, use less liquid. This leaves more flavour in the meat and vegetables so that little, if any, salt is needed. Herbs and spices, lemon juice and various vinegars can also give flavour without recourse to salt.

Where is the salt?

Almost everyone knows that anchovies or potato crisps are salty. But few people realise how much salt comes in some breakfast cereals, savoury biscuits, certain breads or in foods such as cheese. There is nothing wrong with having a few of these foods and if bread is the only salted food you eat, this will not cause any problems. But when every fast food and most prepared foods are laden with salt, the total does become excessive.

No added salt? Salt-reduced? Salt free?

In response to changing palates, many food manufacturers are reducing the added salt in their products. Now for the confusion! 'No added salt' means just that. The only sodium present is that found naturally in the food. Bread with no added salt would have only the sodium from the flour, milk powder (if used) and any grains that have been included.

'Salt-reduced' means salt has been added but in smaller amounts than in the regular product. Salt-reduced breads have 30-60 per cent less salt than that in regular bread.

'Salt free' is an old-fashioned term once used for foods without added salt. As almost all foods have some naturally occurring sodium; the term 'salt-free' is inaccurate and is no longer used.

Different types of salt

Many people pay more for 'sea salt' or 'vegetable salt' assuming they are somehow superior. All forms of salt are sodium chloride and should be used in moderation. Some vegetable salts have a strong flavour (usually from celery extract) so that you can use less of them than regular salt. This may help reduce overall salt intake a little.

Salt substitutes

These products are mostly potassium chloride. Some have other additions to try to take away the bitter after-flavour which about 50 per cent of people experience from potassium chloride. No human population has ever eaten potassium chloride, so we have no long-term safety guidelines. For those who have certain kidney problems, potassium chloride may be harmful. It is probably better to gradually give up using salt and let your taste-buds enjoy the natural flavours of fresh and well-cooked foods.

Mineral water

A few years ago, many mineral waters had a high sodium content. Most have now changed. Look for those brands with less than 70 mg sodium/litre.

Rating the salt in foods (in terms of common servings)

High	*Medium*	*Low*
processed wheat bran	wheat breakfast	rolled oats
cornflakes	biscuits	puffed wheat
processed rice cereal	most mixed cereals	muesli (home-made)
		oat-bran cereals
salted crackers	bread, any type	salt-reduced bread
most canned foods		canned foods with no added salt
	eggs	
	milk	
processed cheese	hard cheese	quark
	cottage cheese	salt-reduced cottage cheese
processed meats	fresh meat	
sausages	chicken	
salami, most		
sandwich meats	turkey	
smoked fish	fresh fish	
fish canned in oil or brine	fish canned in water	
fast foods	home-made hamburger	
prepared foods		
		all fruits
	canned vegetables	frozen or fresh vegetables
potato crisps, snack foods	salted nuts	unsalted nuts
	butter, margarine	unsalted butter or salt-reduced margarine

A Feast of Salads & Vegetables

THE VARIETY OF VEGETABLES AND SALAD ingredients now readily available to us is quite astonishing. Yet, many people still stick to a few old faithfuls, lacking a sense of adventure. Don't miss out on some wonderful tastes and textures. Resolve to try something new next time you visit your greengrocer. With each season, a bountiful supply of vegetables, salad greens and fruits awaits. Check your local markets for the best seasonal buys and choose your recipe accordingly. Many of the dishes in this section need only fresh bread and a juicy fruit dessert to make a complete meal. Some, such as Stuffed Tomatoes or Roasted Red Capsicum Salad, make perfect first courses. Others – Parsley Potatoes or Gingered Snow Peas – are ideal accompaniments to meat or fish courses.

Clockwise from top: Carrot and Hazelnut Salad (page 72), Bean Salad (page 69) and Italian-style Fennel (page 68)   67

Captain James Cook was one of the first people to recognise the need for fresh foods on his ships so his sailors would not get scurvy. He used limes and sprouted wheat grains to produce a fresh source of vitamin C at sea. Vitamin C is needed to make connective tissue which is important in bones, blood capillaries, cartilage, gums and teeth. It also helps to absorb iron from foods, and functions as an antioxidant to help the body's immune system. Breast milk, liver, fruits and vegetables are the only sources.

Stuffed Tomatoes

Serve with crusty bread and salad on their own for a light meal or as a side dish with chicken or meat.

PREPARATION TIME: *10 minutes*
COOKING TIME: *25 minutes*
SERVES 4

4 large tomatoes
3/4 cup cooked green peas
1/2 cup chopped spring onions
1/2 cup cottage cheese
1 teaspoon grainy mustard
2 tablespoons chopped fresh mint
freshly ground pepper
1 tablespoon grated Parmesan cheese

1 Cut a 'lid' from top of each tomato and carefully scoop out contents. Turn tomatoes upside down to drain.
2 Chop the flesh from the tomatoes roughly and place in a small non-stick pan. Boil until thick.
3 Combine cooked tomato flesh with peas, spring onions, cottage cheese, mustard, mint and pepper. Spoon back into tomato shells. Top with Parmesan and bake at 180°C for 10 minutes.

Nutritional information per serve:
Protein 10 g; fat 1 g; carbohydrate 8 g; very good dietary fibre 5 g; 355 kJ (85 Cals)

Other features: An excellent source of vitamin C, a good source of vitamin A, potassium, riboflavin and thiamin, provides useful amounts of niacin and some calcium, iron and zinc. Low sodium (80 mg)

Italian-style Fennel

The slightly aniseed flavour of fennel goes well with grilled or barbecued fish, beef or chicken. Alternatively, use whole baby zucchini or baby eggplant if this flavour is not to your liking.

PREPARATION TIME: *5 minutes*
COOKING TIME: *20 minutes*
SERVES 4

2 teaspoons olive oil
1 medium onion, chopped
1 clove garlic, crushed
425 g can tomatoes
2 large fennel bulbs, cut lengthwise into quarters
1 teaspoon dried basil leaves
2 bay leaves
2 tablespoons chopped parsley

1 Heat oil, add onion and garlic, cover and allow to sweat gently for 2-3 minutes.
2 Add tomatoes, fennel, basil and bay leaves, cover and simmer for 15 minutes, or microwave on High for 6 minutes. Remove bay leaves and sprinkle with parsley.

Nutritional information per serve:
Protein 3 g; fat 2 g; carbohydrate 8 g; very good dietary fibre 7 g; 275 kJ (65 Cals)

Other features: An excellent source of vitamin C, a good source of potassium and provides some iron and vitamin A. Low sodium (80 mg)

Cauliflower Salad with Tahina Dressing

Tahina is made from ground sesame seeds. It has a strong flavour which goes well with this salad. Serve on its own or with grilled lamb kebabs.

PREPARATION TIME: *25 minutes*
COOKING TIME: *Nil*
SERVES 6

1 small cauliflower, left whole
3/4 cup low-fat yoghurt
1 tablespoon orange juice
1 tablespoon tahina
1 small onion, sliced finely
1 teaspoon finely grated orange rind
sprigs of fresh coriander

1 Remove outer leaves and trim stalk on cauliflower. Steam for 10 minutes or microwave on High for 4 minutes (cauliflower should remain crisp). Immediately rinse under cold water. Drain well.
2 Combine yoghurt, orange juice and tahina (if mixture is too thick, add a little more orange juice).
3 Arrange onion rings over cauliflower.

Top with yoghurt mixture and sprinkle with orange rind. Garnish with coriander. Cut into wedges to serve.

Nutritional information per serve:
Protein 5 g; fat 3 g; carbohydrate 6 g; good dietary fibre 3 g; 315 kJ (75 Cals)

Other features: An excellent source of vitamin C and a good source of potassium, riboflavin and thiamin. Also provides some calcium. Low in sodium (45 mg)

Bean Salad

Served with some crisp lettuce, sun-ripened tomatoes and a chunk of fresh wholemeal bread, this salad makes a perfect lunch or summer meal. It is just as lovely the following day, providing the bean sprouts are fresh. Use pre-cooked canned beans that have been drained and rinsed, if preferred.

PREPARATION TIME: *20 minutes + 10 minutes standing time (+ time to soak and cook beans, if not pre-cooked)*
COOKING TIME: *Nil*
SERVES 6

2 cups green beans, cut in halves
1 cup cooked red kidney beans
1 cup cooked butter beans
100 g mushrooms, sliced
1 red and 1 green capsicum, seeded and sliced
1 cup mung-bean sprouts
½ cup parsley

DRESSING
1 clove garlic, crushed
1 teaspoon dried tarragon
1 teaspoon crumbled dried rosemary
2 tablespoons lemon juice
1 tablespoon olive oil
freshly ground black pepper

1 Steam or microwave beans until barely tender. Rinse immediately under cold water and drain.
2 Combine all salad ingredients.
3 Mix all dressing ingredients and pour over salad. Allow to stand for at least 10 minutes before serving.

Nutritional information per serve:
Protein 7g; fat 3 g; carbohydrate 8 g; very good dietary fibre 6 g; 375 kJ (90 Cals)

Other features: Excellent source of vitamin C and provides useful amounts of potassium, and some vitamin A, niacin and iron. Negligible sodium

Sesame Broccoli Salad

This is an ideal salad to serve with grilled chicken, beef, lamb or fish. It can be made ahead if necessary, and refrigerated for an hour or so.

PREPARATION TIME: *25 minutes*
COOKING TIME: *Nil*
SERVES 4

1 tablespoon sesame seeds
500 g broccoli
100 g snow peas, topped and tailed
300 g can baby corn, drained
½ cup sliced spring onions
1 teaspoon sesame oil
2 teaspoons peanut oil
1 tablespoon lemon juice
2 teaspoons salt-reduced soy sauce

1 Toast sesame seeds in a dry frying pan, using a moderate heat and taking care that seeds do not burn. Set aside.
2 Trim broccoli and steam for 3-4 minutes or microwave on High for 2-3 minutes. Immediately run cold water over broccoli. Drain well.
3 Steam snow peas for 1-2 minutes or microwave on High for 1 minute. Run cold water over snow peas and drain well.
4 On serving dish, toss together broccoli, snow peas, baby corn and spring onions.
5 Combine oils, lemon juice and soy sauce. Pour over salad and sprinkle with sesame seeds.

Nutritional information per serve:
Protein 7 g; fat 5 g; carbohydrate 9 g; very good dietary fibre 7 g; 460 kJ (110 Cals)

Other features: Good source of thiamin, riboflavin and potassium and provides some iron, zinc and niacin. Low sodium (80 mg)

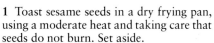

Sesame Broccoli Salad

A real mayonnaise tastes good but it has more than twice the kilojoule level of some processed mayonnaises. Some poly-unsaturated mayonnaises come close to the real thing – at least in kilojoules.

Clockwise from top: Gingered Snow Peas (page 72), Braised Leeks and Potato Bake

Braised Leeks

This is wonderful served hot or cold.

PREPARATION TIME: *5 minutes*
COOKING TIME: *15 minutes*
SERVES 4

¾ cup chicken stock
3 leeks, washed
2 bay leaves
few sprigs of thyme
1 tablespoon olive oil
1 tablespoon wine vinegar
½ teaspoon brown sugar
1 tablespoon chopped parsley

1 Heat chicken stock and boil, uncovered, until reduced by half.
2 Add remaining ingredients, except parsley, to stock. Bring to the boil, cover tightly, turn heat low and simmer for 10 minutes or microwave on High for 6-8 minutes. Remove bay leaves and thyme. Sprinkle with parsley, serve hot or cold.

Nutritional information per serve:
Protein 2 g; fat 5 g; carbohydrate 4 g; good dietary fibre 3 g; 280 kJ (66 Cals)

Other features: Excellent source of vitamin C; provides some iron and potassium. Low sodium (25 mg)

Potato Bake

Traditionally made brimming with butter, this low-fat version tastes delectable, too.

PREPARATION TIME: *25 minutes*
COOKING TIME: *15 minutes*
SERVES 6

½ cup white wine
350 g pumpkin pieces
350 g potatoes, peeled
2 medium green apples, peeled and cored
½ cup low-fat yoghurt
pinch nutmeg
freshly ground black pepper
2 egg whites
1 tablespoon chopped mint

1 Heat wine, add pumpkin, potatoes and apples and cook, covered, until vegetables are tender, or microwave on High for 10 minutes.
2 Mash vegetables, adding yoghurt, nutmeg and pepper.
3 Beat egg whites until stiff and gently fold through vegetable mixture with mint. Pour into a greased ovenproof dish. Bake at 180°C for 15 minutes.

Nutritional information per serve:
Protein 7 g; fat 1 g; carbohydrate 28 g; very good dietary fibre 5 g; 5650 kJ (135 Cals)

Other features: An excellent source of vitamin C, a very good source of vitamin A and potassium and a good source of riboflavin. Provides some calcium. Low sodium (60 mg)

Parsley Potatoes

Few foods are as comforting as hot creamy mashed potato. A microwave takes care of the 'hot' and yoghurt produces a surprisingly creamy consistency.

PREPARATION TIME: *5 minutes*
COOKING TIME: *20 minutes*
SERVES 4

500 g potatoes, peeled
1 cup parsley sprigs
½ cup low-fat yoghurt
1 teaspoon Dijon mustard
freshly ground black pepper

1 Steam potatoes or microwave on High until tender (about 10 minutes).
2 Add parsley and steam or microwave for a further 2 minutes.
3 Drain potatoes and whip potato/parsley mixture with yoghurt and mustard until very smooth and fluffy. Reheat in microwave for 1 minute. Sprinkle with freshly ground pepper.

Nutritional information per serve:
Protein 5 g; no fat; carbohydrate 18 g; good dietary fibre 3 g; 400 kJ (95 Cals)

Other features: An excellent source of vitamin C, a good source of potassium and provides useful amounts of iron and vitamin A. Also has some calcium and niacin. Low sodium (35 mg)

Fruit and vegetables are cheapest when they are in season. That's also when their flavour is at its best. The vitamin C in fruits and vegetables helps you absorb iron from other foods. Another good reason to include a fruit or vegetable at every meal. A well-balanced dinner consists of at least three quarters vegetables and one quarter meat.

Gingered Snow Peas

A simple and superbly-flavoured vegetable dish. Serve it with steamed rice.

PREPARATION TIME: *5 minutes*
COOKING TIME: *15 minutes*
SERVES *4*

3/4 cup chicken stock
1 clove garlic
2 teaspoons sliced fresh ginger
300 g snow peas, trimmed
2 cups sliced mushrooms
1/2 cup sliced spring onions
2 tablespoons dry sherry
1 tablespoon salt-reduced soy sauce

1 Heat chicken stock and garlic and boil until reduced to 1/4 cup. Remove garlic.
2 In a wok or large frypan, place reduced chicken stock, ginger, vegetables and the sherry. Stir-fry for 3-4 minutes, tossing frequently. Add soy sauce. Serve with steamed rice.

Nutritional information per serve:
Protein 6 g; no fat; carbohydrate 8 g; very good dietary fibre 5 g; sodium 155 mg; 230 kJ (55 Cals)

Other features: Very good source of vitamin C, good source of niacin and provides some iron and potassium

Carrot and Hazelnut Salad

This is a wonderful salad which goes well with barbecued seafood or chicken. Do not prepare carrot ahead as it will go brown. Any fresh sprouts can be used.

PREPARATION TIME: *15 minutes*
COOKING TIME: *Nil*
SERVES *4*

1/4 cup chopped hazelnuts
500 g carrots, peeled
1/2 cup sliced spring onions
1 cup sunflower sprouts
1 tablespoon sunflower seeds
1/4 cup orange juice
1 tablespoon extra virgin olive oil
coarsely ground pepper

1 Toast hazelnuts in a dry frying pan over a moderate heat until they are golden brown (be careful they do not burn).
2 Grate carrots, preferably using a food-processor blade to achieve the best texture and appearance. Toss lightly with spring onions, sprouts, sunflower seeds and half the hazelnuts.
3 In blender, combine remaining hazelnuts, orange juice and olive oil. Pour over salad and sprinkle with pepper.

Nutritional information per serve:
Protein 3 g; fat 10 g; carbohydrate 10 g; very good dietary fibre 5 g; 570 kJ (135 Cals)

Other features: Excellent source of vitamin A, very good source of vitamin C and provides useful amounts of potassium. Low sodium (60 mg)

Chick Pea and Avocado Salad

PREPARATION TIME: *20 minutes*
COOKING TIME: *Nil*
SERVES *6*

3 cups cooked chick peas
1 cup cooked green peas
1 red capsicum, seeded and diced
1 avocado, peeled, seeded and diced
selection of lettuce leaves

DRESSING
1 tablespoon extra virgin olive oil
2 tablespoons wine vinegar
1 teaspoon Dijon mustard
1 tablespoon chopped fresh tarragon

1 Combine chick peas, green peas and capsicum.
2 Mix all dressing ingredients together and pour over peas. Let stand for 15 minutes.
3 Add avocado and serve with selection of lettuces.

Nutritional information per serve:
Protein 10 g; fat 14 g; carbohydrate 21 g; excellent dietary fibre 8 g; 1010 kJ (240 Cals)

Other features: Excellent source of vitamin C, good source of iron, potassium, thiamin, niacin. Low sodium (15 mg)

There is no need to wash cultivated mushrooms. If they do not look clean, simply wipe them with a slightly damp cloth. Always store mushrooms in a brown paper or cloth bag. Plastic makes mushrooms sweat and go slimy.

Roasted Red Capsicum Salad

A great salad to make when red capsicums are cheap, plentiful and full-flavoured. Serve it on its own as a first course or with grilled fish, steak or chicken.

PREPARATION TIME: *30 minutes*
COOKING TIME: *Nil*
SERVES 4

4 red capsicums
1 tablespoon pine nuts
2 cups watercress
4 medium tomatoes, very ripe, cut into wedges
1 tablespoon extra virgin olive oil
1 tablespoon balsamic vinegar
1 tablespoon fresh shredded basil

1 For a really sweet flavour, remove skin from capsicums: cut capsicums in half,

remove seeds and place cut side down under a hot grill until skins blister. Place capsicums in a paper bag or wrap in a clean, damp tea towel for 10 minutes. Gently rub off skins. Slice capsicums into strips.
2 Toast pine nuts in a dry frying pan over a low/moderate heat until golden brown. Set aside.
3 Arrange watercress on each serving dish. Arrange tomatoes on half of the watercress and capsicums on the other.
4 Combine oil and vinegar and drizzle a little over each plate. Top with basil and pine nuts.

Nutritional information per serve:
Protein 4 g; fat 5 g; carbohydrate 7 g; good dietary fibre 3 g; 360 kJ (85 Cals)

Other features: Excellent source of vitamin C, good source of potassium and vitamin A and provides some iron and niacin. Negligible sodium

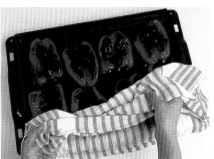

1 Cover blackened capsicums with a clean, damp, tea-towel for about 10 minutes to help remove skin.

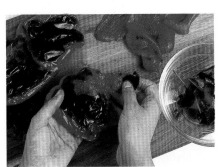

2 Carefully peel away skin from each capsicum, discard blackened skin.

3 Cut peeled capsicum into 2 cm wide strips.

Crunchy Mushroom Salad

PREPARATION TIME: *15 minutes*
COOKING TIME: *10 minutes*
SERVES 6

3 slices wholemeal bread, crusts removed
2 tablespoons extra virgin olive oil
1 clove garlic, crushed
1 tablespoon chopped fresh basil
1 tablespoon chopped fresh parsley
freshly ground black pepper
¼ cup lemon juice
1 teaspoon Dijon mustard
400 g button mushrooms, sliced
1 red capsicum, cut into thin strips

1 Preheat oven to 200°C. Cut bread into 1 cm cubes and place on baking tray. Bake for 10 minutes. Bake at 190°C until crisp and golden. Allow to cool.
2 Mix together oil, garlic, herbs, pepper, lemon juice and mustard in a bowl.
3 Pour over mushrooms and toss gently. Refrigerate for an hour before serving. When ready to serve, sprinkle bread cubes and capsicum on top and serve at once.

Nutritional information per serve:
Protein 4 g; fat 7 g; carbohydrate 7 g; good dietary fibre 3 g; 420 kJ (100 Cals)

Other features: Good source of riboflavin and niacin and supplies some potassium. Low sodium (75 mg)

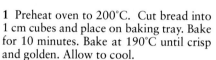

Barbecued Vegetable Kebabs

Read ingredient lists on packaged food. The most prominent ingredient must be listed first, followed by the next major ingredient. Be wary of ingredient lists which include any kind of fat as one of the first three items. Beware the ubiquitous term 'vegetable oil'. Many 'vegetable oils' used in foods are highly saturated fats.

Barbecued Vegetable Kebabs

These vegetable kebabs combine well with barbecued fish or chicken – or they are delicious on their own.

PREPARATION TIME: *15 minutes*
COOKING TIME: *10 minutes*
SERVES 4

8 small Spanish onions, peeled and cut in half
1 red capsicum, cut into 16 squares
1 green capsicum, cut into 16 squares
16 button mushrooms
2 leeks, cut into 2.5 cm pieces
4 thin eggplant, cut into 2.5 cm pieces
1 punnet cherry tomatoes
2 tablespoons low-kilojoule dressing
2 tablespoons chopped fresh herbs (parsley, chives, rosemary or other combinations)

1 Arrange vegetables on skewers (soaked in water to prevent burning).
2 Combine dressing with herbs and brush it over vegetables. Barbecue for about 10 minutes, turning skewers several times and brushing with remaining dressing.

Nutritional information per serve:
Protein 7 g; no fat; carbohydrate 11 g; very good dietary fibre 6 g; sodium 185 mg; 310 kJ (75 Cals)

Other features: Excellent source of vitamin C, good source of potassium, niacin and riboflavin and provides useful amounts of iron and vitamin A

Spicy Green Beans and Walnuts

These beans are delicious served hot but any leftovers are equally good cold with a good chunk of crusty bread.

PREPARATION TIME: *5 minutes*
COOKING TIME: *15 minutes*
SERVES 4

1 tablespoon walnut pieces
500 g green beans, topped and tailed
2 teaspoons walnut oil
1 small onion, chopped finely
¼ teaspoon coarsely ground black pepper
1 teaspoon hot mustard
2 teaspoons paprika
2 tablespoons wine vinegar

1 Toast walnuts in a dry frying pan over a moderate heat until golden brown. Set aside.
2 Steam beans for 5-6 minutes or microwave on High for 4 minutes.
3 While beans are cooking, heat oil and add onion. Cover and allow to cook over a gentle heat for 3-4 minutes. Add pepper, mustard, paprika, vinegar and drained beans. Toss gently and top with walnuts.

Hot Baby Mushrooms and Spicy Green Beans and Walnuts

Nutritional information per serve:
Protein 3 g; fat 4 g; carbohydrate 4 g; good dietary fibre 4 g; 295 kJ (70 Cals)

Other features: An excellent source of vitamin A and also provides some iron and potassium. Negligible sodium

Hot Baby Mushrooms

Serve these mushrooms with a barbecue or grill. Or toss them through a plate of steaming noodles.

PREPARATION TIME: *5 minutes*
COOKING TIME: *10 minutes*
SERVES 4

2 teaspoons olive oil
1 medium onion, sliced
1 clove garlic, crushed
1 teaspoon chopped chilli
2 tablespoons lemon juice
1/2 cup chicken stock
400 g baby mushrooms
1 tablespoon chopped chives

1 Heat oil, add onion, garlic and chilli, cover and leave to sweat for 3-4 minutes.
2 Add lemon juice, stock and mushrooms. Cover and simmer for 5 minutes or microwave, covered, on High for 3 minutes. Sprinkle mushrooms with chives. Serve hot or cold.

Nutritional information per serve:
Protein 4 g; fat 3 g; carbohydrate 4 g; good dietary fibre 3 g; 210 kJ (55 Cals)

Other features: A good source of niacin and riboflavin. Useful amounts of potassium. Low sodium (15 mg)

Microwave cooking gives the best retention of vitamins in cooked vegetables, followed by steaming. Use the minimum amount of water when cooking vegetables so that less flavour is lost and less salt is needed.

Left: Greek-style Zucchini.
Right: Tomato Pie

Tomato Pie

An old-fashioned dish which is always very popular. It looks most attractive and is easy to prepare.

PREPARATION TIME: *15 minutes*
COOKING TIME: *35 minutes*
SERVES 4

3 slices wholemeal bread, made into crumbs
4 or 5 large ripe tomatoes, sliced
1 large onion, sliced
3 medium zucchini, sliced
freshly ground black pepper
¼ cup chopped fresh basil
2 teaspoons butter or margarine

1 Grease an ovenproof pie dish. Sprinkle with 1 tablespoon of the breadcrumbs.
2 Arrange vegetables in layers in dish, sprinkle with pepper.
3 Combine remaining breadcrumbs with basil. Sprinkle over vegetables. Dot with butter or margarine and bake at 180°C for 35 minutes. Serve hot.

Nutritional information per serve:
Protein 5 g; fat 3 g; carbohydrate 15 g; very good dietary fibre 6 g; 380 kJ (90 Cals)

Other features: Excellent source of vitamin C; good source of potassium and also provides useful amounts of iron, riboflavin, niacin and vitamin A. Low sodium (120 mg)

Celeriac with Honey Dressing

The flavour of celeriac resembles celery but the texture is quite different.

PREPARATION TIME: *20 minutes*
COOKING TIME: *Nil*

SERVES 4

1 bulb celeriac (about 400 g)
2 tablespoons lemon juice
1 butterhead lettuce
1 punnet cherry tomatoes

DRESSING
2 tablespoons orange juice
2 teaspoons honey
1 teaspoon Dijon mustard
1/2 teaspoon finely grated orange rind
1 tablespoon tarragon vinegar
1 tablespoon olive oil

1 Peel celeriac and cut into fine strips. Toss with lemon juice to prevent this vegetable turning brown.
2 Combine all dressing ingredients and pour over celeriac.
3 Line a shallow bowl with lettuce leaves, pile celeriac in the centre and decorate with cherry tomatoes.

Nutritional information per serve:
Protein 3 g; fat 5 g; carbohydrate 11 g; very good dietary fibre 7 g; 420 kJ (100 Cals)

Other features: An excellent source of vitamin C, a good source of potassium and provides some riboflavin and niacin. Low sodium (40 mg)

Greek-style Zucchini

For this recipe, the sweet flavour of genuine brown shallot is important. Do not use spring onions.

PREPARATION TIME: *5 minutes*
COOKING TIME: *20 minutes*
SERVES 4

3/4 cup white wine
1/2 cup tomato juice
1 tablespoon lemon juice
1 tablespoon tomato paste
1 teaspoon coriander seeds
1/3 cup raisins
1 bunch brown shallots
600 g small zucchini

1 Combine wine, tomato juice, lemon juice, tomato paste and coriander seeds. Heat gently, cover and simmer 5 minutes, or microwave, covered, on High for 2 minutes.
2 Add raisins, shallots and zucchini, cover and simmer gently for 12 minutes, or microwave, covered, on High for 5 minutes.

Nutritional information per serve:
Protein 4 g; no fat; carbohydrate 15 g; very good dietary fibre 5 g; sodium 130 mg; 335 kJ (80 Cals)

Other features: An excellent source of vitamin C, a good source of vitamin A and potassium and provides useful amounts of iron, riboflavin and niacin

Thai-style Cabbage

This delightfully fresh dish makes a superb accompaniment to steamed rice and fish or chicken. Use prepared chopped ginger and chilli to save time.

PREPARATION TIME: *5 minutes*
COOKING TIME: *15 minutes*
SERVES 4

1 teaspoon oil
1 clove garlic, crushed
2 teaspoons finely chopped lemon grass
1 teaspoon fresh chopped ginger
1/2 teaspoon chopped chilli
2 tablespoons chicken stock
300 g shredded cabbage
1 red capsicum, seeded and sliced
1 cup sliced mushrooms
1 cup snow-pea sprouts (or use bean sprouts)
1 tablespoon chopped mint

1 Heat oil and gently cook garlic, lemon grass, ginger and chilli for 2-3 minutes. Add chicken stock and bring to the boil.
2 Add cabbage, capsicum, mushrooms, sprouts and mint. Toss gently together for 4-5 minutes until thoroughly heated. Serve at once.

Nutritional information per serve:
Protein 3 g; fat 1 g; carbohydrate 4 g; very good dietary fibre 4 g; 150 kJ (35 Cals)

Other features: An excellent source of vitamin C and provides useful amounts of potassium as well as some iron and B vitamins. Low sodium (15 mg)

Thai-style Cabbage

Minerals are added to increase the nutritional value of products such as breakfast cereals, soya bean milk and iodised salt. Some may be present in a form which is not easily absorbed into the body. For example, the iron added to breakfast cereals is not as well absorbed as that in lean meat. Minerals are listed by name and not by number.

ALL ABOUT FIBRE

Dietary fibre was once called 'roughage' and was assumed to be indigestible fibrous material which went in one end of the body and eventually emerged from the other. Dietary fibre is much more complicated than that and undergoes important changes in the intestine. It has a part to play in many areas of health and longevity including the health of the intestine, in diabetes or fluctuating blood-sugar levels, heart disease and cancer. However, not every kind of fibre has equal value in each of these areas.

What is dietary fibre?
Just as there are many different vitamins, each with separate actions to perform in the body, so there are different types of dietary fibre with similarly varied roles. The old term 'roughage' was measured as 'crude fibre' and referred mainly to cellulose – one of the types of dietary fibre. Roughage ignored the pectins, gums, hemi-celluloses and the saponins that all have a bearing on our health. These different types of fibre are found in different foods and you cannot assume your needs are being met just by eating, say, unprocessed bran or an apple a day.

Where is fibre found?
Dietary fibre occurs only in plant foods, including grains, cereals (and foods such as breads and pasta), fruits, vegetables, legumes, seeds and nuts. Meat, fish and dairy products have other important nutrients, but they have no dietary fibre. To get the full range of the different types, you need to select a wide variety of plant foods in your daily meals and your snacks.

What does fibre look like?
You can see strings of fibre in asparagus or spinach stalks, and the grainy fibres in some breads and cereal products. However, the gluey types present in oats and barley do not appear fibrous and if you have ever added pectin to jam to help it set, you will know it is a fine white powder with no obvious fibres. Some foods which look fibrous, such as celery, have very little fibre while others which have no obvious stringiness, such as bananas or potatoes, are good sources of fibre.

How much fibre?
The average daily Western diet has about 15 grams of dietary fibre. By contrast, people in some countries, and many who are vegetarians, have fibre intakes which may be three to four times this level. In general, 30-40 g of fibre a day is recommended.

Soluble and insoluble
Dietary fibres which form a gel when mixed with water or with digestive juices in the intestine are classified as soluble fibres. This includes 'gummy' fibres and hemi-celluloses as well as pectins in fruits. Soluble fibres occur in barley, oats, apples, cabbage and some other vegetables, and in legumes. They can help lower cholesterol, regulate blood sugar levels and help in the prevention of bowel cancer.

Insoluble fibre is found in wholewheat products (wholemeal bread, wholegrain cereals, wheat bran) and in vegetables. It is valuable to prevent constipation and may alter the bacteria in the bowel so that some substances implicated in causing breast cancer are removed from the body.

For good health, try to have a mixture – some soluble and some insoluble fibre.

The digestion of dietary fibre
Dietary fibre is not broken down by the enzymes which digest proteins, fats and carbohydrates in the small intestine. Rather, most types of fibre are digested by bacteria in the large intestine. Soluble fibres are 100 per-cent digested while insoluble ones are digested to varying degrees. Only one type of fibre, lignin, is not digested at all, although it may help remove some substances from the body.

While they are digesting dietary fibre, bacteria produce special acids, called short chain fatty acids. These provide a direct source of energy for the cells in the intestine. One acid causes an electrical stimulation in the bowel wall which helps the muscle wall propel food wastes along the intestine. Another has been shown to stop the action of an enzyme which bowel-cancer cells need in order to multiply.

Constipation
Constipation is more common in women than in men, possibly because many women do not eat enough high-fibre foods. There may also be sex differences in the blood flow to the intestine and in the production of special gut hormones which help move foods along the intestine. A lack of water makes constipation worse.

Regular bowel movements are important but, in fact, it is the consistency of the stools which is more important than frequency. Small, hard stools constitute constipation.

Many people take laxatives. Those containing anthroquinones

(including some herbal laxatives) can damage the nerves in the bowel wall. The bowel is a muscular wall, so regular exercise in moving food along its length is important. Laxatives can destroy muscle tone and should not be used over long periods. A low fibre intake also makes the intestinal muscle walls become slack.

Increasing dietary fibre to 30-40 grams a day and drinking six to eight glasses of water will prevent or cure constipation for most people. Those who have resorted to laxatives over long periods may find they also need the help of a mild faecal softener until their improved diet becomes effective.

Soluble and insoluble fibres work in different ways to increase stool bulk.

Insoluble fibres provide bulk and also absorb water to contribute to the stools. Soluble fibres cause useful bacteria to multiply by the million and their dead bodies are then excreted.

About 70 per cent of the weight of stools represents their water content; the other 30 per cent represents the dead bodies of bacteria which have digested soluble fibre plus some undigested soluble and insoluble fibre.

Flatulence

As bacteria digest fibre, they produce gases. This is normal and when you eat more fibre, you produce more gas. However, if you increase your fibre intake gradually, you will have fewer problems with excessive gas production.

Foods which produce the most gas include legumes, certain vegetables (cabbage, cauliflower, broccoli, Brussels sprouts) and apple juice. Soaking legumes and then discarding the soaking water helps. Eating the clear, outer husk on legumes also helps reduce gas because this coating contains substances which can bind the cause of some of the gas.

Gas and abdominal distension with pain may occur in people who cannot digest milk sugar, or lactose. The natural content of fructose and sorbitol in apple and pear juice also causes excessive 'wind' in some people.

Dietary fibre content of foods

Food	Fibre (g)
Vegetables, av. serve of any	1
Beans, kidney or baked, 1 cup cooked	18
Peas, average serve	5
Sweet-corn kernels, 1 cup	7
Fruit, average piece	3
Fruit, dried, 50 g	9
Nuts or seeds, 30 g	3
Coconut, fresh, 75 g	10
Peanut butter, 30 g	3
Bread	
white, 2 slices	2
multigrain, 2 slices	3
wholemeal, 2 slices	5
rye, 2 slices	3
Cereals (average bowl)	
bran, mixed cereal,	11
bran, processed wheat	9
branflakes	7
cornflakes, rice bubbles	1
mixed cereals (flakes and fruit)	3
muesli, natural	5
porridge (rolled oats)	4
Bran, unprocessed, 2 tablespoons	6
Wheat biscuits, 2	4
Wheatgerm, 1 tablespoon	2
Barley, cooked, 1 cup	4
Pasta, cooked	
white, 2 cups	4
wholemeal	9
Rice, cooked, 1 cup	
white	2
brown	3
Wheat, cracked, cooked, 1 cup	5

How to change from a low-fibre to a high-fibre diet

Low-fibre choices	High-fibre choices
Breakfast	
Cornflakes	Rolled oats, wheat biscuits or bran cereal
White toast with honey	Wholemeal toast with marmalade
Morning tea	
Coffee and biscuits	Coffee and wholemeal fruit loaf
Lunch	
Chicken sandwich/ white bread	Chicken and salad sandwich/ wholemeal bread
Apple, peeled	Apple, with peel
Afternoon snack	
Chocolate bar	Banana
Dinner	
Grilled steak	Grilled steak
Chips	Jacket potato
Green salad	2 or 3 vegetables
Ice-cream	Fruit salad
Total	*Total*
11 g fibre	41 g fibre

Delicious Desserts & Cakes

HERE LIES THE DOWNFALL OF MANY A HEALTHY EATER! But don't despair if you love cakes and desserts. You don't have to live your life without them. There are many recipes which fall into the category of healthy as well as delectable, that use only a fraction of the fat, sugar and kilojoules needed in traditional recipes. Some of those featured here do contain sugar – they would be lacking in all-important flavours without it. But, only the minimum amount consistent with producing a good product has been used. Indulge family and friends (and yourself, of course) with Ricotta Cheesecake or Raspberry Ice-cream. Lovers of comfort food, please note. There's plenty for you, too. Try Steamed Peach Pudding with Orange Sauce or home-style Fruit Crumble and discover that sweet treats can do you a power of good!

Lemon Heart with Berries (page 82) and Ricotta Cheesecake (page 82)

Lemon Heart with Berries

This is a light dessert which can be served in any season. Vary the type of berries according to the seasons and your taste.

PREPARATION TIME: *20 minutes + 3 hours setting time*
COOKING TIME: *Nil*
SERVES 6

2 teaspoons gelatine
1 tablespoon water
1 tablespoon lemon juice
250 g ricotta cheese (low-fat)
1 cup low-fat yoghurt
1 egg white
2 tablespoons caster sugar, or use artificial sweetener

FRUIT TOPPING
1 punnet strawberries
1 punnet blueberries
1 tablespoon rum (optional)

1 Soften gelatine in water. Add lemon juice and heat gently until gelatine dissolves, or microwave on High for 30 seconds.
2 Beat together ricotta, yoghurt and gelatine mixture.
3 Beat egg white until stiff, adding sugar or sweetener. Gently fold into ricotta mixture. Rinse a heart-shaped tin with cold water. Pour ricotta mixture into tin, refrigerate for 2-3 hours.
4 Hull strawberries and slice. Mix with blueberries and rum and allow to stand, covered, for at least 30 minutes.
5 Turn heart out of tin and top with the strawberries and blueberries.

Nutritional information per serve:
Protein 9 g; fat 3 g; carbohydrate 10 g (or 16 g if sugar is used); some dietary fibre 2 g; 450 kJ (110 Cals), 575 kJ (135 Cals) if sugar is used

Other features: A good source of vitamin C and calcium. Useful amounts of potassium. Low sodium (120 mg)

Ricotta Cheesecake

This cake is half-way between a moist cake and a baked cheesecake in texture. It is delicious served with puréed raspberries or puréed apricots (fresh or canned).

PREPARATION TIME: *15 minutes*
COOKING TIME: *40 minutes*
SERVES 8

2 egg whites
2 tablespoons sugar
500 g ricotta cheese (low-fat)
1 tablespoon honey
2 tablespoooons plain flour
1 teaspoon finely grated lime or lemon rind
1 tablespoon lime or lemon juice
1/2 cup low-fat yoghurt
2 egg yolks
1/2 teaspoon bitters

1 Beat egg whites until peaks form. Add sugar and continue beating until stiff. Gently tip egg whites on to a plate.
2 Using the same bowl (no need to wash), combine remaining ingredients and beat until smooth.
3 Fold in egg white mixture, place in a paper-lined 20 cm cake tin and bake at 180°C for 40 minutes.

Nutritional information per serve:
Protein 9 g; fat 6 g; carbohydrate 11 g; no dietary fibre; sodium 145 mg; 550 kJ (130 Cals)

Other features: A good source of calcium

Banana Whip

This amazing dessert surprises everyone. It's simply frozen bananas, whipped. Can be kept in the freezer for a couple of days.

PREPARATION TIME: *10 minutes + freezing time*
COOKING TIME: *Nil*
SERVES 6-8

6 bananas

1 Peel bananas, place on a tray lined with plastic wrap and freeze for several hours.

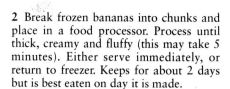 

2 Break frozen bananas into chunks and place in a food processor. Process until thick, creamy and fluffy (this may take 5 minutes). Either serve immediately, or return to freezer. Keeps for about 2 days but is best eaten on day it is made.

Nutritional information per serve:
Protein 2 g; no fat; carbohydrate 23 g; good dietary fibre 3 g; 420 kJ (100 Cals)

Other features: Good source of vitamin C

Almond Bread

This wonderful bread is made in two stages. It has no added fats. Serve with fresh fruit at dessert or with tea or coffee at afternoon tea. It does contain some sugar but the quantity in each slice works out at less than half a teaspoon.

PREPARATION TIME: *15 minutes + 10 minutes*
COOKING TIME: *20 minutes + 10 minutes*
MAKES *40 slices*

4 egg whites
1/2 cup caster sugar
1 cup plain flour
1 cup almonds
1/2 teaspoon vanilla essence

1 Beat egg whites until stiff. Fold in caster sugar and continue beating until shiny.
2 Gently fold in the flour, almonds and vanilla. Spoon mixture into a well-greased loaf tin. (If tin is not a non-stick variety, line it with baking paper.) Bake at 180°C for 30 minutes.
3 Tip loaf out. Allow to cool completely. Store in an airtight container for at least 12 hours.
4 Using a very sharp knife, cut loaf into very thin slices. Place on ungreased oven trays and bake at 150°C for about 10 minutes or until lightly browned (be careful not to burn).

Nutritional information per slice:
Protein 1 g; fat 2 g; carbohydrate 5 g; small amount of dietary fibre 1 g; 180 kJ (42 Cals)

Other features: Negligible sodium (6 mg)

Grecian Oranges

Served well chilled, these oranges are the perfect foil for a rich dinner. They can also be prepared ahead. This dessert is free of all fat, and does not need added cream or ice-cream. If desired, omit sugar and add artificial sweetener.

PREPARATION TIME: *20 minutes + chilling time*
COOKING TIME: *Nil*
SERVES *4*

4 oranges
1 cup water
1/2 cup sugar
2 tablespoons brandy

1 Using a potato peeler or a very sharp knife, cut the peel from 2 of the oranges, taking care not to include any white pith. Slice peel into fine strips.
2 Cover orange-peel strips with water, bring to the boil and simmer gently for 10 minutes. Drain and rinse well.
3 Combine water and sugar (see Note) and bring to the boil. Add drained peel and simmer for about 5 minutes or until peel looks clear. Using a slotted spoon, remove peel from syrup and reserve.
4 Peel and remove pith from remaining oranges. Add oranges to syrup and simmer for 2 minutes. Add brandy. Cool then chill well. Serve each orange in a glass dish and top with orange shreds.
Note If desired, omit sugar and sprinkle cooked peel with artificial powdered sweetener. Add more artificial sweetener, to taste, when adding brandy.

Nutritional information per serve:
Protein 2 g; no fat; carbohydrate 43 g (or 18 g if artificial sweetener used); good dietary fibre 4 g; 800 kJ (190 Cals) or 380 kJ (90 Cals) if sweetener used

Other features: An excellent source of vitamin C. Also provides some vitamin A and potassium. Negligible sodium

Ask yourself if a food is worth the fat and kilojoules before you take the second bite. If you avoid eating the pastry on a fruit pie, you save around 1500 kJ (360 Cals). An average iced doughnut has 1425 kJ (340 Cals). An average packet of potato chips has 740 kJ (175 Cals) and 11 grams of fat. One croissant has as many kilojoules as 3 slices of toast.

Champagne Mangoes, Raspberry Ice-cream and Almond Bread (page 83)

Champagne Mangoes

This is the king of all desserts – simple and delicious. Make sure the mangoes are well chilled. If you want to avoid alcohol, use freshly squeezed orange juice instead.

PREPARATION TIME: *15 minutes*
COOKING TIME: *Nil*
SERVES 4

4 medium mangoes
1 tablespoon Cointreau or Grand Marnier
1 cup champagne
sprigs mint

1 Peel mangoes and cut slices from each.
2 Combine Cointreau and champagne. Pour over mango slices, leave for 10 minutes. Decorate each serve with a sprig of mint and serve with Almond Bread.

Nutritional information per serve:
Protein 1 g; no fat; carbohydrate 17 g; some dietary fibre 2 g; 525 kJ (125 Cals)

Other features: An excellent source of vitamins C and A and a useful source of potassium. Sodium negligible

Raspberry Ice-cream

This rich-tasting ice-cream gives no indication of its low fat content. Served with fresh berries, it makes an excellent dessert.

PREPARATION TIME: *15 minutes + 1-4 hours freezing, depending on equipment*
COOKING TIME: *Nil*
SERVES 6

2 cups skim milk
½ cup evaporated skim milk
1 cup skim-milk powder
1 tablespoon cornflour
1 teaspoon vanilla essence
⅓ cup sugar or use artificial powdered sweetener
1 punnet raspberries (or strawberries)

1 In blender or food processor, combine all ingredients except raspberries.
2 Place in saucepan and heat gently, stirring continuously until mixture boils and thickens. Cool slightly.

3 Add raspberries and freeze in an ice-cream churn, following the manufacturer's directions. Or freeze until edges are solid, beat in an electric mixer and re-freeze until mixture is solid.

Nutritional information per serve:
Protein 13 g; no fat; carbohydrate 33 g (or 21 g if sweetener used); good dietary fibre 3 g; sodium 200 mg; 780 kJ (185 Cals) or 580 kJ (140 Cals) if sweetener used.

Other features: A very good source of riboflavin and a good source of potassium. Rich in calcium

Coffee Cream Pots

One of the simplest desserts which tastes rich and creamy, but is quite low in fat.

PREPARATION TIME: *10 minutes + at least 1 hours refrigeration*
COOKING TIME: *Nil*
SERVES 6

500 g ricotta cheese (low-fat)
2 tablespoons strong coffee (use decaffeinated if desired)
¼ cup caster sugar or use artificial powdered sweetener
pinch cinnamon
1 tablespoon brandy
1 tablespoon finely shredded orange rind
¼ cup water

1 Using an electric mixer, combine all ingredients except orange rind. Whip until very smooth. Place in 6 small individual dishes and refrigerate for at least an hour.
2 Place orange rind in a small saucepan with ¼ cup water. Boil for 2 minutes. Drain. Use to decorate the dessert.

Nutritional Information per serve:
Protein 10 g; fat 6 g; carbohydrate 11 g (or 2 g if using sweetener); no dietary fibre; sodium 165 mg; 650 kJ (155 Cals) or, if using sweetener, 500 kJ (120 Cals)

Other features: A good source of calcium

Freeze cream in ice-cube containers. This makes it easy to have just a tablespoon of cream to enrich a sauce without being tempted to use up the whole container.High quality, commercial ice-creams taste good but they have about 16 per cent fat compared with 10 per cent fat in regular ice-cream. One ice-cream cone has 80 kJ (19 Cals). 2 scoops of ice-cream have 750 kJ (180 Cals).

Coconut and Almond Kulfi

This slightly sticky Indian-style ice-cream is rich in calcium. It is delicious served after a simple curry. You will not need to eat much as it is so rich.

PREPARATION TIME: *15 minutes + 1-3 hours freezing time, depending on equipment*
COOKING TIME: *Nil*
SERVES 6

2 cups skim milk
1 cup skim-milk powder
1/2 cup evaporated skim milk
1 tablespoon custard powder
1/3 cup desiccated coconut
1/3 cup sugar (or use equivalent in powdered sweetener)
1/3 cup almonds, chopped roughly
2 teaspoons finely grated orange rind
1 teaspoon vanilla essence

1 In a saucepan combine milks, custard powder and coconut. Stir continuously over a low heat until mixture boils and thickens.
2 Add sugar (or sweetener), almonds, rind and vanilla. Place mixture into an ice-cream churn and follow manufacturer's directions. Alternatively, freeze in a shallow dish until completely frozen, beat and re-freeze. Serve in small portions with sliced mango or other fresh fruit.

Nutritional information per serve:
Protein 14 g; fat 6 g; carbohydrate 32 g (or 20 g if sweetener used); some dietary fibre 2 g; sodium 195 mg; 990 kJ (225 Cals) or 795 kJ (190 Cals) if sweetener is used

Other features: An excellent source of riboflavin and a good source of potassium. Rich in calcium

Lemon Mousse with Strawberry Sauce

A smooth, not-too-sweet mousse served with a tangy fruit sauce, this makes a delightful summer dessert.

PREPARATION TIME: *20 minutes + 2 hours setting time*

COOKING TIME: *Nil*
SERVES 6

1 tablespoon gelatine
2 tablespooons lemon juice
1/4 cup boiling water
1 tablespoon honey
500 g low-fat yoghurt
375 mL evaporated skim milk
1 teaspoon very finely grated lemon rind

STRAWBERRY SAUCE
1 punnet strawberries
1 tablespoon rum
2 tablespoons low-kilojoule strawberry jam

1 Soften gelatine in lemon juice. Dissolve in boiling water. Add honey or sweetener.
2 Combine yoghurt, milk and rind. Add gelatine mixture and stir thoroughly. Pour into a mould which has been lightly oiled.
3 To make sauce, place all ingredients in a blender and process until smooth. If preferred, sieve to remove 'pips'.

Nutritional information per serve:
Protein 13 g; no fat; carbohydrate 21 g (or 15 g if using sweetener); sodium 175 mg; 610 kJ (145 Cals) or 525 kJ (125 Cals) with sweetener

Other features: An excellent source of riboflavin, a good source of potassium, niacin and vitamin C. Rich in calcium

Strawberry Shortcake

The yoghurt and lemon in this cake give it body and moistness. It keeps well for a day or two. Diabetics should have a very small portion only.

PREPARATION TIME: *15 minutes*
COOKING TIME: *25 minutes*
SERVES 8

3 tablespoons flaked almonds
1 cup wholemeal self-raising flour
1/3 cup cornflour
1/2 cup dark brown sugar
1 egg, beaten
1 teaspoon finely grated lemon rind
1 cup low-fat yoghurt
1 punnet strawberries
1 tablespoon brandy

Cow's milk has more vitamin E, vitamin B$_{12}$ and folate (one of the B vitamins) than goat's milk. Fat, protein and carbohydrate levels are similar. Sheep's milk has about one-and-a-half times the protein and fat levels of cow's milk.

1 Grease a 20 cm non-stick cake tin and sprinkle 2 tablespoons of the almonds over the base.
2 Combine all ingredients except strawberries and brandy. Spoon mixture over almonds. Bake at 190°C for 25 minutes.
3 While shortcake is cooking, slice strawberries and sprinkle with brandy. Serve with wedges of the cake.

Nutritional information per serve:
Protein 5 g; fat 3 g; carbohydrate 23 g; good dietary fibre 3 g; sodium 170 mg; 630 kJ (150 Cals)

Other features: Provides some potassium

Pumpkin Loaf

This well-flavoured loaf is delicious served warm. It contains honey but the quantity is small and the dietary fibre present makes it suitable for diabetics.

PREPARATION TIME: *10 minutes*

COOKING TIME: *45 minutes*
MAKES *18-20 slices*

3/4 cup cooked mashed pumpkin
1/4 cup oil
1/3 cup honey
2 eggs, beaten
1 teaspoon cinnamon
1/2 teaspoon ground ginger
1/2 teaspoon nutmeg
2 cups wholemeal self-raising flour
1 teaspoon baking powder
2/3 cup evaporated skim milk

1 In food processor, combine all ingredients and mix well.
2 Pour into a paper-lined, non-stick loaf tin and bake at 180°C for 45 minutes. Turn out and cool. Serve cut into thin slices with smooth ricotta cheese whipped with a little cinnamon.

Nutritional information per slice:
Protein 4 g; fat 4 g; carbohydrate 14 g; some dietary fibre 2 g; sodium 175 mg; 465 kJ (110 Cals)

Left: Coconut and Almond Kulfi. Right: Strawberry Shortcake

Steamed Peach Pudding with Orange Sauce

A steamed pudding with minimum fat but a surprisingly good flavour and texture.

PREPARATION TIME: *10 minutes + 30 minutes standing*
COOKING TIME: *1 hour*
SERVES 4

1 teaspoon butter or margarine
4 slices smooth wholemeal bread, without crusts
½ cup chopped dried peaches
1 cup skim milk
1 tablespoon honey
2 eggs
1 teaspoon finely grated orange rind
½ teaspoon vanilla essence

SAUCE
1 cup orange juice
1 tablespoon cornflour
1 tablespoon orange juice, extra
1 tablespoon brandy

1 Butter a small pudding basin.
2 Cut each slice of bread into cubes (do not cut through all slices at once, or bread will be doughy). Combine with peaches.
3 Beat together milk, honey, eggs, rind and vanilla. Pour over bread and leave for 20 minutes.
4 Pour pudding mixture into greased basin, cover with buttered foil and secure with string. Place in a saucepan with enough water to come half-way up sides of pudding basin. Steam for 1 hour. Turn out and serve with sauce.
5 To make the sauce, heat juice until almost boiling.
6 Blend cornflour with extra juice and brandy. Stir into hot juice and cook for 1-2 minutes.

Nutritional information per serve (including sauce):
Protein 8 g; fat 4 g; carbohydrate 33 g; good dietary fibre 4 g; sodium 190 mg; potassium 420 mg; 860 kJ (205 Cals)

Other features: Good source of vitamin C; a good source of riboflavin and of iron. Provides useful amounts of calcium and potassium

Steamed Peach Pudding with Orange Sauce

1 Pour combined milk, honey, eggs, orange rind and vanilla over bread and peaches.

2 Place pudding mixture into greased pudding basin.

Don't skip breakfast – it gets your metabolism going and helps you burn up more kilojoules during the entire day. For those who skip lunch and have a 4 p.m. chocolate 'attack': a typical chocolate bar has as many kilojoules as three-and-a-half salad sandwiches.

3 Place a layer of greased foil over pudding basin, tie the foil securely with string.

4 Stir blended cornflour, extra juice and brandy into hot juice, stir constantly until thickened.

Oat Biscuits

Once you acquire a taste for these oat biscuits, they become irresistible. Delicious served with low-fat Cheddar or light cream cheese.

PREPARATION TIME: *10 minutes*
COOKING TIME: *15 minutes*
SERVES 8

1 cup quick-cooking oats
1/2 teaspoon bicarbonate soda
1/2 teaspoon cinnamon
25 g butter or margarine
1 tablespoon water
1 tablespoon honey

1 Combine dry ingredients.
2 Heat butter or margarine, water and honey until margarine melts. Pour into dry ingredients and mix well to make a dough.
3 Knead dough and pat to a 20 cm circle. Mark into 8 wedges. Place dough on a non-stick baking tray and bake at 180°C for 15 minutes or until lightly brown and crisp. Serve warm with a low-fat spread, honey, jam or cheese.

Nutritional information per oat biscuit:
Protein 2 g; fat 3 g; carbohydrate 11 g; small amount of dietary fibre 1 g; 340 kJ (80 Cals)

Other features: Low sodium (26 mg)

Fruit Rounds

Another delightful recipe for children to make. Scrumptious served with coffee or an ideal snack when out sailing, walking or picnicking.

PREPARATION TIME: *20 minutes*
+ refrigeration time
COOKING TIME: *Nil*
MAKES *about 48 rounds*

1 cup dates
1 cup sultanas
1 cup raisins
1/2 cup currants
3/4 cup (100 g) chopped nuts
1/4 cup sunflower seeds
1/2 cup dessicated coconut

2 tablespoons lemon juice
1 tablespoon extra coconut, toasted in dry pan until brown

1 Mince fruits and nuts together (or grind in food processor). Add remaining ingredients and mix well.
2 Using wet hands, shape mixture into 2 logs. Roll them in extra coconut. Wrap in plastic wrap and refrigerate for several hours before cutting into slices to serve.

Nutritional information per round:
Protein 1 g; fat 1 g; carbohydrate 7 g; small amounts of dietary fibre 1 g; 170 kJ (140 Cals)

Other features: Negligible sodium

Apricot Squares

This is always a favourite recipe for children to make as it needs no baking.

PREPARATION: *25 minutes + refrigeration*
COOKING TIME: *Nil*
MAKES *about 48*

1 cup chopped dried apricots
3/4 cup sultanas
1/2 cup chopped prunes, pitted
1/2 cup orange juice
1 cup skim-milk powder
1/2 cup fresh wholemeal breadcrumbs
1/2 cup chopped almonds
1/4 cup desiccated coconut

1 Combine apricots, sultanas, prunes and orange juice. Bring to the boil, cover and leave to stand for 15 minutes.
2 Add milk powder, breadcrumbs and almonds and mix thoroughly.
3 Sprinkle half the coconut over the base of a non-stick shallow pan about 25 cm x 18 cm. Press mixture into pan and sprinkle with remaining coconut, pressing it in well. Cover and leave in refrigerator for several hours before cutting into small squares to serve.

Nutritional information per square:
Protein 2 g; fat 1 g; carbohydrate 5 g; small amounts of dietary fibre 1 g; 145 kJ (35 Cals)

Other features: Low sodium (20 mg)

Sugar by another name: sucrose, glucose, dextrose, lactose, maltose and fructose are all sugars. Sorbitol and mannitol are sugar alcohols which have as many kilojoules as sugar. Sorbitol is not suitable for diabetics. Diabetes is not caused by eating sugar. However, once diabetes appears, sugar consumption must be limited.

Fruit Crumble

Use any pie-pack fruit on hand for this dish. Pie-pack fruit has been blanched and canned immediately. The can contains 100 per cent fruit – no sugar, syrup or additives. Using a food processor, it is a fast and easy hot dessert.

PREPARATION TIME: *10 minutes*
COOKING TIME: *20 minutes (or 12-15 using microwave)*
SERVES 4

50 g butter or margarine
1/2 cup brown sugar
1 teaspoon cinnamon
1 cup rolled oats
1/2 cup crunchy oat bran
1 tablespoon sunflower seeds
1 tablespoon sesame seeds
410 g pie-pack peaches, apricots or apples

1 In a food processor, combine all ingredients except fruit.
2 Place fruit in a casserole dish and pour crumble mixture on top. Press down with your fingers or the back of a spoon. Bake at 180°C for 20 minutes or microwave on High for 12-15 minutes. Serve with a vanilla sauce.

Nutritional information per serve:
Protein 5 g; fat 14 g; carbohydrate 38 g; good dietary fibre 4 g; 1240 kJ (295 Cals)

Other features: Useful source of iron. Low in sodium (16 mg)

Fruit Crumble

Remember the microwave for making porridge. Place some oats in your bowl, add some skim milk, stir and cook on High for 2 minutes. No dirty saucepan to wash.

Raisin Oat Bread

A beautifully flavoured loaf which is also great toasted.

PREPARATION TIME: *15 minutes*
COOKING TIME: *45 minutes*
MAKES *1 loaf, about 18 slices*

2 1/2 cups wholemeal self-raising flour
1 cup rolled oats
1 teaspoon bicarbonate of soda
1 tablespoon brown sugar
3/4 cup raisins
300 g low-fat yoghurt
1/2 cup orange juice

1 Combine all dry ingredients and raisins.
2 Add yoghurt and juice and mix to a soft dough. Bake in a loaf tin or knead on a floured surface until smooth and place on a non-stick ovenproof tray. Bake at 180°C for 40-45 minutes or until the loaf has risen and sounds hollow when it is tapped underneath.

Nutritional information per slice:
Protein 4 g; fat 1 g; carbohydrate 18 g; some dietary fibre 2 g; sodium 160 mg; 420 kJ (100 Cals)

Wholemeal Lemon Pikelets

Whip up a quick batch of healthy pikelets for a Sunday afternoon treat. You won't find out how well these keep as they will always disappear very quickly.

PREPARATION TIME: *15 minutes*
COOKING TIME: *10 minutes*
MAKES *about 30*

2 cups wholemeal plain flour
1 tablespoon sugar
2 eggs, separated
1 1/2 cups low-fat milk
1 tablespoon lemon juice
1 teaspoon finely grated lemon rind

1 Mix together flour, sugar, egg yolks, milk, juice and rind.
2 Beat egg whites until stiff. Fold in flour mixture.
3 Heat a non-stick pan until hot. Cook spoonfuls of the mixture until bubbles appear. Turn and cook other side until golden brown. Serve warm with whipped ricotta cheese or light cream cheese, or with a little lemon juice.

Nutritional information per pikelet:
Protein 2 g; fat 1 g; carbohydrate 6 g; small amounts of dietary fibre 1 g; 150 kJ (35 Cals)

Other features: Sodium negligible (11 mg)

Clockwise from left: Oat Biscuits (page 89), Raisin Oat Bread and Wholemeal Lemon Pikelets

Apricot Almond Loaf

Cardamom adds an intriguing taste to cakes. This one keeps well and is sweet enough without sugar.

PREPARATION TIME: *15 minutes + 30 minutes cooling time*
COOKING TIME: *35 minutes*
MAKES *16 slices*

200 g dried apricots
1 cup orange juice
1 egg
1/2 cup skim milk
2 teaspoons finely grated lemon rind
1/2 cup roughly chopped almonds
1/2 cup wheatgerm
1 cup wholemeal self-raising flour
1/2 teaspoon baking powder
1/2 teaspoon ground cardamom (or use cinnamon)

1 Place apricots and juice in a saucepan and bring to the boil. Cover and leave to stand until cooled slightly.
2 Combine egg, milk, rind, almonds and apricots and mix well.
3 Add wheatgerm, sifted flour, baking powder and cardamom, tipping bran from sifter into mixture.
4 Pour into a greased loaf tin and bake at 180°C for 35 minutes. Turn out and cool before serving.

Nutritional information per slice:
Protein 3 g; fat 3 g; carbohydrate 10 g; a very good source of dietary fibre 5 g; 340 kJ (80 Cals)

Other features: Useful amounts of potassium and some iron. Low sodium (64 mg)

A banana has more than twice as much dietary fibre as a typical green salad. Make a delicious low-fat afternoon tea for children by peeling a banana, wrapping it in plastic wrap and freezing it.

Banana and Carrot Muffins

A wonderful weekend breakfast or great for afternoon tea. Serve these hot from the oven and you won't need to add butter.

PREPARATION TIME: *15 minutes*
COOKING TIME: *20 minutes*
MAKES *12*

1 large carrot
2 bananas, peeled
1 tablespoon dark brown sugar
2 eggs
1/4 cup low-fat yoghurt
1 teaspoon cinnamon
1 1/3 cups wholemeal flour
2 teaspoons baking powder
1/2 cup unprocessed bran

1 Using a food processor, shred carrot finely (there will be 1 cup of carrot, firmly packed).
2 Add bananas, sugar, eggs, yoghurt and cinnamon to food processor and whizz until well blended.
3 Sift flour and baking powder into banana mixture, tipping husks out of sifter into the mixture. Add unprocessed bran and mix quickly (do not overmix).
4 Place mixture into 12 greased muffin pans. Bake at 200°C for 20 minutes. Serve the muffins warm.

Nutritional information per muffin:
Protein 4 g; fat 1 g; carbohydrate 15 g; good dietary fibre 4 g; 375 kJ (90 Cals)

Other features: Provides some calcium and potassium. Low sodium (95 mg)

Banana and Orange Scones

PREPARATION TIME: *20 minutes*
COOKING TIME: *15 minutes*
MAKES *10-12 scones*

2 small bananas
1 teaspoon finely chopped orange rind
2 tablespoons skim-milk powder
1 egg
1 tablespoon low-fat butter or margarine
2 tablespoon orange juice
1/4 teaspoon cardamom
2 cups wholemeal self-raising flour
1/2 teaspoon baking powder

1 In food processor, mix bananas, rind, milk powder, egg, butter or margarine, orange juice and cardamom. (Or mash bananas and mix well with other ingredients.)
2 Sift flour and baking powder into

banana mixture, tipping bran and germ into mixture from sifter. Mix lightly to a dough.

3 On a floured board, pat out to a circle and cut out 10-12 round scones. Place on a greased tray and bake at 200°C for 12-15 minutes. Serve warm.

Nutritional information per scone:
Protein 4 g; fat 2 g; carbohydrate 18 g; good dietary fibre 3 g; sodium 235 mg; 460 kJ (110 Cals)

Other features: Provides some calcium and potassium. Low sodium (95 mg)

Clockwise from left: Banana and Orange Scones, Apricot Almond Loaf and Banana and Carrot Muffins

ALL ABOUT SUGAR

Breast milk is rich in the sugar called lactose. Although lactose is not as sweet as regular sugar, it may well be the cause of many people's lifetime love affair with sweetness. It is also likely that our early ancestors discovered that sweet-tasting foods were generally safe to eat while bitter foods were often found to be poisonous.

Natural?

Sugars occur in nature in many different forms. Milk has lactose, sugar-cane has sucrose, fruit has fructose, sprouting grains and malt have maltose, honey has a mixture predominantly of fructose but with some glucose and sucrose also present. In the context of their original food, any one of these forms of sugar could be called 'natural'.

However, the term 'natural' is not applicable when sugars are extracted from their natural source and concentrated to a level quite unlike their form in nature. It is probably fair to say that the high level of refined sugar consumed in most Western countries would be impossible to ingest from any sugar source in its natural form. Sugar-cane, for example, has so much fibre that no one could take in the huge amounts of sugar which are possible by consuming refined sugar. Nor could we ever chew our way through enough fruit to supply the quantity of fructose which we can easily obtain from fruit juices or from extracted fructose. In nature, most sugars come with dietary fibre – a natural obstacle to overeating. The exceptions are honey and the sugar in milk. But, as honey is hard to find in nature and milk contains less than 4 per cent sugar, a high intake of these sugars is unlikely in practice.

Is sugar bad?

Nutritionally, refined sugar has no protein, minerals, vitamins, essential fatty acids or dietary fibre. Most foods with a lot of added sugar have little in the way of the important nutrients. Some people argue that sugar increases consumption of healthy foods such as breakfast cereals. But sugar also makes fats taste nice. Most of us would not eat chocolate, cakes, biscuits, pastries, ice-cream or desserts if sugar did not sweeten up their greasy fats.

If used in addition to a healthy diet, moderate quantities of sugar probably do little damage to most people, providing they brush their teeth after eating sweet foods. In many Western countries, annual consumption of sucrose is around 50 kg per person, or almost a kilogram a week. Such a high average is not 'moderate'.

Diabetics and those with raised levels of triglycerides must keep sugar consumption low. It also makes sense for those who are overweight to cut back on sugar. Several committees have looked at the health effects of sugar and concluded that, apart from its impact on dental decay, it is not solely responsible for any major health problems. But, we must not minimise the effect of sugar on teeth; this is in itself a major health problem.

The major factor in eating sugar is 'moderation'. Some recipes cannot be made without it but many dishes can be made with much less of it – especially if they contain the natural sweetness and flavour of fresh fruits.

Sugar and energy

Blood sugar, or blood glucose, is a major energy source for all body cells. We do not need to eat refined sugar because the body can easily convert all carbohydrates to glucose. Proteins, either from food or from lean muscle tissue, can also be broken down to glucose. Fats cannot be changed to glucose although excess sugar or glucose in the blood can easily be changed to fat.

The body strives to maintain blood-glucose levels within normal limits because the brain needs glucose as fuel. Those with fluctuating blood-sugar levels or hypoglycaemia may have a slight delay in restoring high or low blood-glucose levels to normal. In untreated diabetes, the level of blood glucose rises because glucose cannot move into the cells in the absence of insulin. If glucose 'spills over' into the urine, the blood-glucose level may become dangerously low.

When blood-glucose levels drop, the body mobilises some glucose stored in the liver as liver glycogen. A hunger pang is often the first signal of a slight drop. If you don't eat, the body quickly uses some of its stored liver glycogen to replenish blood glucose and the hunger pang goes away for a while. Once that blood sugar is used, you feel another hunger pang and the process is repeated. Stores of liver glycogen are limited and after a few hunger pangs the body starts to break down its lean muscle tissue. This happens if you skip a meal or deliberately fast, have no food, or have untreated diabetes. It makes sense to eat enough carbohydrate to keep blood-glucose levels normal so that lean muscle tissue is not used to replenish them.

Any carbohydrate can contribute to blood glucose but it is best to eat those which are also suppliers of the important nutrients such as vitamins, minerals and dietary fibre. Fruits, breads, cereals, grains and vegetables such as potatoes and sweet corn are all good for keeping blood-glucose levels normal.

Sugar can also restore blood-sugar levels but in the case of large quantities, the excess will be converted into body fat.

Hypoglycaemia (low blood sugar)

A drop in blood sugar occurs in most people several times a day, usually two to five hours after a meal. As mentioned above, this stimulates appetite and we eat and restore blood-sugar levels. This is normal. Hypoglycaemia can also be reversed by breaking down some lean muscle tissue and converting the protein to blood glucose.

Some people react to the normal temporary 'lows' in their blood-glucose levels by feeling a sudden loss of energy. This often happens about 4 p.m. Symptoms may include irritability, inability to make decisions, headache, feelings of shakiness, depression, poor concentration, increased sweating or nausea. It is possible to 'iron out' blood-sugar-level fluctuations by eating smaller meals with between-meal snacks of high-fibre carbohydrate foods. Eating more lunch, or dividing lunch into two portions and leaving some to eat halfway through the afternoon, seems to help.

Candida

A similar set of the symptoms ascribed to hypoglycaemia is also blamed on *Candida albicans*, a yeast-like fungus. Candida normally live on human skin and are found in the mouth, vagina and intestinal tract. Almost everyone given a 'candida test' will have a positive result, just as we would all test positive for the many bacteria and fungi with which we cohabit. In itself, this does not represent a health problem nor a disease condition.

Some believe candida multiply when the diet contains sugar, white bread or any yeast-containing food such as yeast extract, cheese, wine or beer. An anti-candida diet which omits these foods is then prescribed. There is no scientific evidence that this diet works. Where it seems to be effective, it may be that the person was sensitive to some other food chemicals such as amines which are present naturally in some foods. Or, the expectation that the diet will work may give a positive psychological result. The lack of refined sugar in the anti-candida diet presents no problem since sugar is not essential, or even useful. However, some of the other foods omitted can cause nutritional gaps in the daily diet.

Other sugars

Apple-juice concentrate is a popular substitute for sugar. It is simply another form of sugar. Unless apple-juice concentrate gives a particular texture, there is no nutritional reason to use it because the goodness of fruit – largely its fibre – is gone.

Glucose

Some people take glucose for 'instant energy', especially before physical activity. The energy in muscles for physical activity depends on the carbohydrates consumed at least 12 hours beforehand. Glucose will raise blood-sugar levels but may also stimulate an outpouring of insulin which will then cause them to fall again. Any excess glucose can also be converted to body fat. Glucose is useful for people in hospital after surgery. It is a waste of money for most other people and certainly for athletes.

Honey

Honey is a natural sugar but nature intended it for bees, not humans. The quantities of minerals and vitamins in most honeys are ample for a small bee but insignificant in a human diet. Honey is very sweet so it can sometimes be used in smaller quantities than sugar to provide a sweet flavour.

Raw sugar, molasses, demerara sugar

Molasses is the least refined form of sugar from sugar-cane. It has some iron and calcium but there are few data on how well these are absorbed. Raw sugar is quite highly refined and has insignificant quantities of nutrients. Demerara sugar is a raw sugar with molasses added to provide colour. Each of these sugars may give particular flavours but they have no special health benefits.

Health Shakes & Little Extras

THERE ARE ALL SORTS OF RECIPES that make healthy eating a pleasure that don't fit into one or other of the sections we've covered here. So, this is a lovely mix of ideas that will brighten your day from breakfast to dinner. Breakfast is a most important meal and often gets neglected in the morning rush. But, it takes so very little time to whip up a low-fat breakfast drink. These health shakes are also ideal for active, growing children who need something to eat between meals. Banana Smoothie or Peach Cooler should prove popular. If you've a little more time to spare, Banana Bran Pancakes or a special Muesli will get your day off to a healthy start.

Clockwise from top: Apricot Almond Delight (page 98), Pink Drink (page 102), Peach Cooler (page 98), Banana Smoothies (page 99) and Muesli (page 98)

Muesli

Unlike purchased toasted mueslis, this one has no added fat. You can purchase the roasted buckwheat and pepitas at a health food shop.

PREPARATION TIME: *30 minutes*
COOKING TIME: *Nil*
MAKES *about 45 serves (40 g each)*

750 g rolled oats
1 cup barley flakes
1 cup rye flakes
1/2 cup sesame seeds
1 cup wheatgerm
2 cups processed oat-bran cereal
1/2 cup roasted buckwheat
250 g dried-fruit medley
250 g sultanas
1/2 cup sunflower seeds
1/2 cup pepitas

1 Place half the oats on an ungreased oven tray, bake at 200°C for about 10-15 minutes, stirring several times, until golden brown. Alternatively, microwave on High for 10 minutes. Repeat with remaining oats and barley. Cool all grains.
2 Toast sesame seeds in a dry frying pan until golden brown (take care they do not burn). Cool.
3 Combine all ingredients and store in an airtight container.

Nutritional information per serve:
Protein 4 g; fat 4 g; carbohydrate 24 g; good dietary fibre 4 g; 610 kJ (145 Cals)

Other features: A good source of thiamin and provides some iron, zinc and potassium. Sodium negligible

Apricot Almond Delight

This is a refreshing and filling drink with an interesting flavour.

PREPARATION TIME: *5 minutes*
COOKING TIME: *Nil*
SERVES 2

5 or 6 fresh apricots (or use canned apricots without sugar)
250 mL orange juice
200 g low-fat yoghurt
1 tablespoon flaked almonds
2 or 3 ice-cubes
grated nutmeg

Place all ingredients in blender and process until well mixed. Sprinkle with nutmeg before serving.

Nutritional information per serve:
Protein 8 g; fat 4 g; carbohydrate 29 g; very good dietary fibre 5 g; 750 kJ (180 Cals)

Other features: An excellent source of vitamin C, a very good source of vitamin A and potassium, a good source of calcium, thiamin and riboflavin. Provides some iron and niacin. Low sodium (85 mg)

Peach Cooler

Try using apricot juice instead of peach.

PREPARATION TIME: *5 minutes*
COOKING TIME: *Nil*
SERVES 2

1 cup canned peach juice
1 cup buttermilk
2 tablespoons skim-milk powder
3 or 4 ice-cubes

Place all ingredients in blender and process until well mixed.

Nutritional information per serve:
Protein 8 g; fat 2 g; carbohydrate 24 g; no dietary fibre; sodium 125 mg; 610 kJ (145 Cals)

Other features: A very good source of riboflavin and thiamin, a good source of calcium and potassium

Buttermilk is no longer a by-product of butter-making but is a low-fat milk product thickened slightly with a bacterial culture. It is similar to, but not as thick as yoghurt. Use it in scones, baking or added to cold soups instead of milk or cream. Skim milk is an acquired taste for some. If you are having trouble getting used to it, try mixing it half and half with regular milk, and gradually increase the proportion of skim milk.

Banana Smoothies

An old favourite and always popular with all ages. The added wheatgerm makes it even more nutritious. Low-fat milks make frothier shakes than regular milk. Substitute 1 piece of rockmelon, pawpaw or 150 g of blueberries or strawberries for banana if desired.

PREPARATION TIME: *5 minutes*
COOKING TIME: *Nil*
SERVES *1*

1 glass skim milk
½ cup low-fat yoghurt
1 banana
1 teaspoon honey (optional)
1 tablespoon wheatgerm
2 or 3 ice-cubes
few drops vanilla

Place all ingredients in blender and process until fluffy.

Nutritional information per serve:
Protein 14 g; fat 2 g; carbohydrate 41 g (or 36 g if honey omitted); good dietary fibre 4 g; 990 kJ (235 Cals) or 905 kJ (215 Cals) without honey; sodium 175 mg

Other features: An excellent source of riboflavin, a very good source of potassium and a good source of thiamin and vitamin C. Also provides useful amounts of zinc. Rich in calcium

Cracked Wheat Bread

This dark, heavy bread is delectable served in very thin slices. It needs no kneading.

PREPARATION TIME: *10 minutes + soaking and standing time*
COOKING TIME: *1 hour*
MAKES *about 30 slices*

½ cup cracked wheat
½ cup cracked or whole rye grain
¼ cup linseeds
300 mL hot water
600 mL warm water
750 g wholemeal plain flour
½ teaspoon salt
3 x 7 g sachets dried yeast

Cracked Wheat Bread

1 Soak cracked wheat, rye and linseeds overnight in 300 mL hot water.
2 Next day, add remaining ingredients and mix well. Leave to stand for 3-4 hours. (In cold weather, cover bowl with plastic wrap.)
3 Pour into a heavy-duty, well-greased bread tin and bake at 200°C for 1 hour. Tip out and leave to cool thoroughly before cutting in very thin slices to serve.

Nutritional information per slice:
Protein 4 g; fat 1 g; carbohydrate 18 g; good dietary fibre 3 g; 420 kJ (100 Cals)

Other features: A good source of thiamin and provides some niacin and iron. Low sodium (33 mg)

Researchers have shown that sugar-sweetened soft drinks do not quench your thirst. Water or soft drinks sweetened with Aspartame both quench thirst – and have no kilojoules.

Ricotta Fruit Whip

This is a good substitute for whipped cream with only a fraction of the fat. You can make it up to an hour before serving.

PREPARATION TIME: *5 minutes*
COOKING TIME: *Nil*
SERVES 6

1 cup ricotta cheese
2 tablespoons concentrated orange juice
1 cup canned pears in pear juice, drained
1/2 teaspoon vanilla essence

Place all ingredients in a blender and process until very smooth.

Nutritional information per serve:
Protein 6 g; fat 4 g; carbohydrate 6 g; dietary fibre 1 g; 335 kJ (80 Cals)

Other features: Useful source of vitamin C and calcium. Low sodium (95 mg)

Banana Bran Pancakes

For a delicious weekend breakfast, make up the mixture for these pancakes the night before. Make sure you use a very hot pan for best results. Leftover mixture can be stored in the refrigerator for the following day, if desired.

PREPARATION TIME: *15 minutes*
COOKING TIME: *10-15 minutes*
SERVES 6

2 cups skim milk
1 tablespoon lemon juice
1 large or 2 small ripe bananas
1 cup wholemeal flour
1/2 cup unprocessed bran
1 egg, separated
cinnamon

1 In blender, combine all the ingredients except egg white and cinnamon. Leave to stand in refrigerator overnight.
2 In the morning, beat egg white until stiff, fold into pancake mixture.
3 Heat a non-stick pan, grease it lightly and pour about one sixth of mixture into pan. Swirl to spread mixture. Cook about

Prepared breakfast cereals may have anything from no sugar to over 50 per cent sugar. Check the side of the packet before buying. Some breakfast cereals are so nutritious that they make ideal snacks or desserts for hungry children, or light meals at any time of the day.

1 minute, turn and cook other side. Sprinkle with cinnamon and serve.

Nutritional information per pancake:
Protein 8 g; fat 2 g; carbohydrate 23 g; very good dietary fibre 5 g; 580 kJ (140 Cals)

Other features: A good source of riboflavin and thiamin, provides useful amounts of calcium, potassium and niacin and some iron. Low sodium (55 mg)

Apricot and Ginger Sauce

Pie-pack fruit has been blanched and canned immediately. The can contains 100 per cent fruit – no sugar, syrup or additives.

PREPARATION TIME: *10 minutes*
COOKING TIME: *15 minutes*
SERVES 6

400 g pie-pack apricots
1 teaspoon chopped ginger
1/2 cup white wine
1/2 cup orange juice
1 tablespoon cornflour
sweetener to taste
1 tablespoon brandy (optional)

1 Heat apricots with ginger and wine.
2 Blend orange juice and cornflour and stir into apricot mixture. Cook for 1-2 minutes, stirring constantly. Add sweetener and brandy if desired.
3 Purée sauce until smooth. Serve warm or chilled.

Nutritional information per serve:
No protein; no fat; carbohydrate 8 g; dietary fibre 1 g; 185 kJ (45 Cals)

Other features: Good source of vitamin C and a useful source of vitamin A. Negligible sodium (5 mg)

Banana Bran Pancakes served with Ricotta Fruit Whip and Apricot and Ginger Sauce

Calcium has little effect on energy but greatly influences the density of bones. A lack of calcium – like iron – is mainly a problem for women. To keep bones strong, try to have some calcium-rich foods every day. Milk, yoghurt and cheese are excellent sources and you can avoid their fat by using low-fat varieties. Other sources of calcium include fish with edible bones (such as canned sardines or salmon), almonds, fortified soya bean milk, tofu (soya bean curd), tahina (the pale-coloured kind made with hulled sesame seeds), oranges and green vegetables. Some of the low-fat fortified milks are concentrated sources of calcium – excellent products for women's needs.

Pink Drink

A great favourite with children who love the pretty colour.

PREPARATION TIME: *10 minutes*
COOKING TIME: *Nil*
SERVES 2

*1 slice watermelon (about 250 g) with
pips removed
2 bananas
¹/₂ punnet strawberries
1 cup buttermilk*

Place all ingredients in blender and process until well mixed.

Nutritional information per serve:
Protein 8 g; fat 3 g; carbohydrate 33 g; very good dietary fibre 5 g; 775 kJ (185 Cals)

Other features: An excellent source of vitamin C, a very good source of thiamin, a good source of calcium, potassium and riboflavin and provides some iron. Low sodium (72 mg)

Herb Sauce

This is an ideal sauce to serve with fish or chicken. It does need fresh herbs. You can vary the herbs used here.

PREPARATION TIME: *5 minutes*
COOKING TIME: *10 minutes*
SERVES 4

*1 cup chicken stock
1 piece lemon peel, about 5 cm
1 clove garlic, peeled
1 tablespoon chopped fresh parsley
1 tablespoon chopped fresh coriander
1 tablespoon chopped fresh thyme
1 tablespoon cornflour
¹/₄ cup evaporated skim milk
freshly ground pepper*

1 Heat chicken stock with lemon peel and garlic. Simmer, covered, for 2 minutes. Remove lemon peel and garlic. Add herbs.
2 Mix cornflour with evaporated milk. Add to hot stock, stirring constantly until sauce boils and thickens.

Nutritional information per serve:
Protein 2 g; no fat; carbohydrate 5 g; less than 1 g dietary fibre; 130 kJ (30 Cals)

Other features: Low sodium (45 mg)

Spiced Raisin Sauce

This sauce is a good accompaniment to pork, veal or poultry.

PREPARATION TIME: *5 minutes*
COOKING TIME: *25 minutes + 30 minutes
standing time*
SERVES 6

*1 cup apple juice
¹/₄ cup red wine
4 cardamom pods
1 cinnamon stick, about 8 cm
6 cloves
1 piece orange peel, about 10 cm
1 cup raisins
2 teaspoons arrowroot or cornflour
2 tablespoons water
1 tablespoon lemon juice*

1 Heat apple juice, wine and spices until boiling. Cover and leave for 30 minutes. Strain off liquid, retaining liquid and discarding spices and peel.
2 Add raisins to liquid, bring to the boil and simmer 10 minutes, or microwave, covered, on High for 4 minutes.
3 Blend arrowroot or cornflour with water. Add to raisin mixture, stirring constantly until mixture boils and thickens. Add lemon juice.

Nutritional information per serve:
No protein; no fat; carbohydrate 22 g; some dietary fibre 2 g; 360 kJ (85 Cals)

Other features: Some niacin, potassium and vitamin C. Low sodium (20 mg)

Tangy Lemon Sauce

A simple tangy sauce which is lovely served with fresh asparagus, broccoli or with seafoods.

PREPARATION TIME: *5 minutes*
COOKING TIME: *15 minutes*
SERVES 4

2 teaspoons Dijon mustard
1/2 teaspoon dried ground tarragon
1/4 cup white wine vinegar
1/4 cup lemon juice
1 egg, beaten
freshly ground black pepper
few drops of sweetener

1 In a small saucepan, mix mustard and tarragon. Add vinegar and lemon juice. Bring to the boil.
2 Stirring constantly, gradually add beaten egg to lemon mixture. Cook over a low heat until thickened. Add pepper and sweetener to taste.

Nutritional information per serve:
Protein 1 g; fat 1 g; no carbohydrate; no dietary fibre 85 kJ (20 Cals)

Other features: Low sodium (20 mg)

Home-made Tomato Sauce

Once you taste home-made tomato sauce, it is hard to go back to the purchased varieties. It must be stored in the refrigerator in hot weather.

PREPARATION TIME: *10 minutes*
COOKING TIME: *20 minutes*
MAKES 4 1/2 cups

2 teaspoons olive oil, preferably extra virgin
1 medium onion, chopped roughly
1 clove garlic, crushed
1/2 teaspoon dry mustard
1 kg ripe tomatoes, chopped roughly
3/4 cup tomato purée
2 bay leaves
1 teaspoon dried oregano
freshly ground black pepper

1 Heat oil, add onion and garlic, cover and cook over a gentle heat for 3-4 minutes. Add mustard and cook a further 1 minute.
2 Add remaining ingredients, bring to the boil, cover and simmer for 10-15 minutes. Cool a little, purée until smooth. If desired, strain sauce through a sieve to remove tomato seeds. Bottle and store in the refrigerator.

Nutritional information per 1/4 cup:
No protein; no fat; carbohydrate 2 g; dietary fibre 1 g; 55 kJ (13 Cals)

Other features: Useful source of vitamin C. Low sodium (40 mg)

Fruit Salad Sauce

A most refreshing sauce. Serve it with low-fat ice-cream or as a dip for fresh fruits.

PREPARATION TIME: *10 minutes*
COOKING TIME: *Nil*
SERVES 4

1/4 rockmelon
1 mango
4 apricots
1 kiwi fruit, peeled
1/2 cup orange juice
3 passionfruit

Peel and seed rockmelon, mango and apricots and place fruit flesh in blender with kiwi fruit and juice. Process until smooth. Stir in passionfruit pulp.

Nutritional information per serve:
Protein 2 g; no fat; carbohydrate 14 g; very good dietary fibre 5 g; 270 kJ (65 Cals)

Other features: An excellent source of vitamin C, very good source of vitamin A and provides useful amounts of potassium. Sodium negligible (10 mg)

A lack of iron is a common cause of fatigue and lack of energy in women. Iron is needed for making haemoglobin, a pigment in red blood cells which carries oxygen to every cell in the body. If you do not have enough haemoglobin, less oxygen is delivered to each cell. The cells are then unable to produce their full potential energy level. The result, naturally, is a feeling of tiredness. Iron comes in two forms: haem iron in meat, fish and chicken; and non-haem iron in vegetables, grains, legumes, nuts, seeds and eggs.

ALTERNATIVE DIET STRATEGIES

There are many types of vegetarian diets. Some provide the best possible selection of nutrients; others can lead to malnutrition. There are also 'semi' vegetarian diets which include fish and chicken but avoid red meat. As with all diets, the adequacy of any vegetarian diet depends on the variety and quantities of foods selected. Other 'alternative' diets are described and discussed below.

Lacto-ovo vegetarian

These diets include eggs, milk, yoghurt and cheese as well as a range of grains, legumes, seeds, nuts, fruits and vegetables.

A major advantage of any vegetarian diet is its high fibre content. But lacto-ovo vegetarian diets can still be high in fat, especially if considerable amounts of fried foods, chocolate, cheese and high-fat dairy products are used. Fibre will give protection against some of the harmful effects of too much fat, but cannot overcome them completely. It is also easy to kid yourself a meal is healthy just because it seems light and avoids meat. For example, a slice of spinach quiche and salad can have about six times as much fat and less dietary fibre than a piece of lean steak and some vegetables.

A lacto-ovo vegetarian diet can, in theory, provide all the necessary nutrients. The most common problem it raises occurs with women who are at risk of a lack of iron – a nutrient well supplied by meat. Legumes, grains and green vegetables can supply iron to meet even the high requirements of women, but many women omit legumes and eat insufficient quantities of valuable foods such as wholemeal bread and vegetables, thus depriving themselves of iron. Iron supplements can help but some cause constipation.

Children whose parents believe in a lacto-ovo vegetarian diet generally have few nutritional problems. However, it is important to allow them to have regular milk, yoghurt, eggs and some cheese as well as a variety of fruits, vegetables, legumes, grains,

seeds and ground nuts or nut butters such as peanut butter. For some children, a vegetarian diet may contain so much fibre that they develop loose motions. In such cases, use white rice, white bread and white pasta occasionally instead of wholemeal all the time.

Vegan diet

This is the true vegetarian diet and it omits all animal products. Legumes, grains, seeds, nuts, fruits and vegetables have to supply all nutrients. As long as enough is eaten and there is plenty of variety, a vegan diet can be quite adequate for an adult.

For children and those needing a high kilojoule intake (such as endurance sportspeople), a vegan diet can present difficulties. Small children may not be able to sit at a table long enough to eat sufficient food to meet their high growth needs and the high fibre content of the diet may be too much for their small intestinal tract. Athletes may be unable to devote the time and chewing effort necessary to eat the large bulk of food needed to fuel their very high kilojoule requirements. And, for those who do manage to eat enough, the high bulk and dietary fibre may be a problem.

In practice, vegans often don't eat enough and are likely to be low in nutrients such as calcium and iron. Foods such as almonds, soy products, soy yoghurt and tahina can help increase calcium while legumes, grains and green vegetables will supply iron.

Vitamin B_{12} occurs mainly in animal products so can be in short supply in a vegan diet. Mushrooms and the fermented soy

products such as tempeh can provide some B_{12} and some medical researchers believe the vitamin may be made by bacteria within the intestine. Contrary to popular belief, comfrey does not contain an active form of vitamin B_{12}. As it contains dangerous alkaloids, it should be avoided. Pregnant women on vegan diets should take supplementary B_{12}.

Food combining

There is a popular theory that the body cannot digest proteins and carbohydrates at the same time. Its adherents maintain that some foods should not be combined.

What this theory does is ignore the facts of digestion. In the small intestine, many litres of digestive juices are produced and these contain the enzymes to break down proteins, fats and carbohydrates at the same time. If this were not the case, we would be unable to digest cereals, grains, nuts, seeds or legumes – all natural foods which each contain protein and carbohydrate. Most of the world's population survives very healthily on these foodstuffs – without digestive problems.

The food-combining theorists may be confused between the roles of the stomach and the small intestine. Indeed, some entirely ignore the small intestine – an important omission since almost all digestion occurs there. The stomach acts more as a holding chamber and gradually releases its contents to the small intestine. Carbohydrates tend to leave the stomach fastest, followed by proteins and then fats. This does not mean that all protein waits in the stomach until the carbohydrates have departed. There is considerable overlap, in fact, and the body is perfectly well able to handle foods containing each of these nutrients.

It may be more important to try to eat certain foods together rather than as separate items. For example, eating a fruit which contains vitamin C with foods such as wholemeal bread or legumes helps in the absorption of iron from the bread or legumes.

No fat, no cholesterol, no sugar, no salt, no alcohol

Many people have adopted a spartan approach to diet and religiously avoid fat, cholesterol, sugar, salt and alcohol. As well as following this strict dietary approach, some people also increase their amount of exercise in order to achieve reduced blood-cholesterol levels, weight loss, falls in high blood pressure and blood-triglyceride levels.

Such extreme approaches certainly work but a modified approach is likely to produce equally good results for most people.

Diets such as the Pritikin program are not suitable for infants and young children. Breast milk derives 50 per cent of its kilojoules from fat; it also contains cholesterol. These are important to the rapidly growing infant and a sudden change to a diet with 10-15 per cent of its kilojoules coming from fat is too drastic for one so young. During periods of rapid growth and relatively small capacity for food, fat is an important concentrated source of kilojoules.

Eating is also an important social aspect of life. There are many delicious recipes which fit the very strict criteria of the Pritikin lifestyle – some are included in this book. Unfortunately, such a diet can make eating out in restaurants and with friends very difficult. The task of finding the right foods can then dominate life.

While there are no nutritional hazards in striving for minimum levels of sugar, salt and alcohol, the effort to reduce fat to minimal levels can lead to a lack of minerals such as iron, calcium and zinc. Some essential fatty acids may also be low in diets which restrict the consumption of all foods containing fat.

There is no doubt that fatty diets are unhealthy. The balanced solution may be to have very little fat and to make sure that it is of high value. Foods such as fish, very lean meat or poultry and a little olive oil can supply essential fats without making the level of fat in the diet too high.

Macrobiotic diets

Like vegetarian diets, a macrobiotic diet can be a healthy choice or it may lack certain nutrients. This depends on the type and quantity of foods chosen.

A macrobiotic diet aims to create a balance between 'yin' and 'yang'. Yin represents the negative, passive, and, some claim, feminine, side of life, whereas yang is positive, strong and masculine. Foods are classified as either yin or yang and a desirable balance of five parts yin to one part yang is said to promote health and balance of mind and body. Factors such as climate, exercise, stress and state of health are taken into account in deciding the ideal balance for individuals.

At the centre of yin and yang are vegetables and cereals. These foods form the bulk of the macrobiotic diet. The foods which are highly yin include sugar, liquids of all kind, alcohol, fruit and dairy products. Chemicals and drugs are also regarded as yin. Yang foods are meat, fish, poultry, eggs and salt. Very few raw fruits, raw vegetables or liquids are suggested.

Miso soup, made from fermented soy beans, salt and brown rice plays a prominent role in the macrobiotic diet and is believed to contain enzymes which assist the digestion.

The macrobiotic diet is actually a series of diets ranked according to various levels. The initial levels consist of a fairly wide selection of foods with the greatest emphasis being placed on vegetables, wholegrains with some fish, meat or poultry. Such a diet can be nutritionally well-balanced. The ultimate level (usually the seventh or tenth level) is brown rice only and a ten-day diet of brown rice is recommended at frequent intervals to 'cleanse' the body. Brown rice is supposed to have the ideal balance of yin and yang. Liquids are severely limited.

Nutritionally, the early levels of macrobiotic diets can be quite well-balanced. However, this diet may easily be inadequate for children and the high salt content of miso is unwise for those with or at risk of high blood pressure.

The brown-rice level is nutritionally unbalanced and quite inadequate. It would lead to various nutrient deficiencies and death if followed for long.

ALL ABOUT WEIGHT

Body weight is made up of skin, bone, muscle, water and fat. The only undesirable element of the mix is an excess level of fat. We need some body fat but not too much. Deciding how much fat is enough and what is excessive can be difficult. Many men who are too fat for the sake of their health are quite unconcerned about their spreading girth while many women who fear that they are overweight, are not.

Where is the fat?

Excess fat is a health hazard when it accumulates on the abdomen and upper body – the typical 'apple-shape'. Fat in these regions increases the risk of coronary heart disease, high blood pressure, diabetes, gallstones and cancers of the breast and bowel. Fat on the hips, bottom and thighs – 'pear-shape' – is much less of a health hazard and is not related to any of these conditions.

Types of fat

Fat around the middle of the body is present in large fat cells which can become so stuffed with fat that they feel hard. Some men mistake this 'tyre' for muscle or dismiss it as being a 'beer gut'. It is neither of these; it is, in fact, hazardous fat.

Fat on the thighs and bottom is often in very small fat cells which frequently clump together, forming the familiar 'cellulite'. This does not represent 'toxic wastes', poor digestion or a sluggish metabolism, as is sometimes claimed by those who promote methods to suck it out, rub it off or sweat it away. Cellulite is simply fat which is not supported by enough muscle to hold it firmly in place. Exercise, not diet or miracle 'cures', is the way to help cellulite.

Diets

Most diets work on the principle of weight loss rather than fat loss. It is much easier to reduce weight by losing water or muscle than it is to burn off excess body fat. However, it is worse than useless to lose weight by reducing the body's normal content of water or

muscle. Water is essential for every reaction in the body and muscle burns up many kilojoules. Those who lose muscle need to consume fewer kilojoules than those who retain or increase their lean muscle tissue.

Whenever a diet lacks sufficient carbohydrate, there will be a loss of muscle and water. This is the basis of many popular diets, especially those which promise fast and/or easy weight loss. These diets restrict the intake of carbohydrate foods such as bread, potatoes, rice and grains. Studies have shown that 85 per cent of the weight loss with these diets is water; 10 per cent is muscle and only about 5 per cent of the lost weight is related to fat.

Fat loss is a much slower process than the fast diets promise. It is difficult for anyone to lose more than one kilogram of fat a week and most people will not lose more than 0.5 kg. Bear in mind that this represents the amount of fat in a regular-sized tub of margarine.

Fats in foods are converted to body fat much more easily than carbohydrates. The latter are used preferentially for energy for physical activity. Therefore, an ideal fat-loss diet is low in fat and restricts carbohydrates to a much lesser extent.

Ten top tips to judge a well-balanced diet program

- It is designed for a weight loss of 0.5-1.0 kg a week
- It has a variety of foods so that it does not become boring
- It is as close as possible to the types of foods you can afford and will be able to buy and prepare
- It can be followed without having to buy special foods
- It represents a change in eating habits which you could follow forever
- It encourages exercise
- It does not claim secret ingredients or combinations of foods (there is none)
- It has been designed by someone with recognised dietetic qualifications
- It is not too expensive
- It provides support or back-up when you need it

The following day's menu is to give you an idea of a well-balanced way to eat to give a weight loss of 0.5-1.0 kg per week. Remember to walk or do some other extra exercise for 20-30 minutes, preferably about five days a week.

Sample menu

Breakfast
Fresh fruit – 1 piece
Wholegrain cereal – moderate serve with low-fat milk (avoid sugar)
Wholemeal toast – 1-2 slices with low-fat spread and low-kilojoule jam, yeast extract or sliced tomato
Tea or coffee or water or low-fat milk

Lunch
Wholemeal sandwich (no butter or margarine) with filling of lots of salad plus salmon, tuna, chicken or cottage cheese
Fresh fruit – 1-2 pieces
Water or mineral water

Dinner
Grilled fish or chicken or very lean meat (small serve)
Potato or rice or pasta (without butter or cream)
Plenty of vegetables, any kind
Fresh fruit or fruit salad, or fruit canned without sugar – moderate serve only

Between meals
Skim milk – 1 cup (made into milk shake with ice-cubes, vanilla or coffee and sweetener, if desired) or small carton low-fat natural yoghurt
1 piece fresh fruit
If desired:
1 slice of wholemeal bread or raisin bread or half a muffin with low-fat spread
Extra piece fresh fruit
This menu supplies 5000-6500 kJ (1200-1550 Cals) and is nutritionally balanced.

Underweight
Those who are overweight find it hard to believe, but it can be more difficult for the thin person to gain weight than it is for the overweight to lose it.

Most people who are underweight are smokers, do not eat regularly or are small eaters. Some may consume a great deal in public but follow this with long periods of eating little. A few are underweight because they follow some fad diet which prohibits many foods. Some boys are also thin for a while and this may follow a growth spurt. Most eat large quantities of food and eventually find that they will gain some weight.

Tips to gain weight
- Do not smoke
- Eat meals and snacks between meals. If you have difficulty consuming a lot at any one time, eat many times during the course of the day
- Exercise in moderation; avoid extremes
- Nibble nuts (they are not too filling)
- Drink enriched milk shakes (see recipe section)
- Avoid too many high-fibre foods which are filling
- Wait – time inevitably 'cures' the problem for many people

USEFUL INFORMATION

The recipes in this book are all thoroughly tested,
using standard metric measuring cups and spoons.
All cup and spoon measurements are level.
We have used eggs with an average weight of 55 g each
in all recipes. In this book, metric measures and their imperial
equivalents have been rounded out to the nearest figure that is easy to
use. Different charts from different authorities vary slightly; the
following are the measures we have used consistently throughout our
recipes.

OVEN TEMPERATURE CHART

	°C	°F	Gas Mark
Very slow	120	250	1/2
Slow	150	300	1–2
Mod. slow	160	325	3
Moderate	180	350	4
Mod. hot	190	375	5–6
Hot	200	400	6–7
Very hot	230	450	8–9

LENGTH

Metric	Imperial
5 mm	1/4 in
1 cm	1/2 in
2 cm	3/4 in
5 cm	2 in
8 cm	3 in
10 cm	4 in
12 cm	5 in
15 cm	6 in
20 cm	8 in
25 cm	10 in
30 cm	12 in
46 cm	18 in
50 cm	20 in
61 cm	24 in

CUP & SPOON MEASURES

A basic metric cup set consists of 1 cup, 1/2 cup, 1/3 cup and 1/4 cup sizes.

The basic spoon set comprises 1 tablespoon, 1 teaspoon, 1/2 teaspoon and 1/4 teaspoon.

1 cup	250 mL/8 fl oz
1/2 cup	125 mL/4 fl oz
1/3 cup (4 tablespoons)	80 mL/ 2 1/2 fl oz
1/4 cup (3 tablespoons)	60 mL/2 fl oz
1 tablespoon	20 mL
1 teaspoon	5 mL
1/2 teaspoon	2.5 mL
1/4 teaspoon	1.25 mL

LIQUIDS

Metric	Imperial
30 mL	1 fl oz
60 mL	2 fl oz
100 mL	3 1/2 fl oz
125 mL	4 fl oz (1/2 cup)
155 mL	5 fl oz
170 mL	5 1/2 fl oz (2/3 cup)
200 mL	6 1/2 fl oz
250 mL	8 fl oz (1 cup)
300 mL	9 1/2 fl oz
375 mL	12 fl oz
410 mL	13 fl oz
470 mL	15 fl oz
500 mL	16 fl oz (2 cups)
600 mL	1 pt (20 fl oz)
750 mL	1 pt 5 fl oz (3 cups)
1 litre (1000 mL)	1 pt 12 fl oz (4 cups)

DRY INGREDIENTS

Metric	Imperial
15 g	1/2 oz
30 g	1 oz
45 g	1 1/2 oz
60 g	2 oz
75 g	2 1/2 oz
100 g	3 1/2 oz
125 g	4 oz
155 g	5 oz
185 g	6 oz
200 g	6 1/2 oz
250 g	8 oz
300 g	9 1/2 oz
350 g	11 oz
375 g	12 oz
400 g	12 1/2 oz
425 g	13 1/2 oz
440 g	14 oz
470 g	15 oz
500 g	1 lb (16 oz)
750 g	1 lb 8 oz
1 kg (1000 g)	2 lb

GLOSSARY

burghul = cracked wheat
capsicum = sweet pepper
cornflour = cornstarch
eggplant = aubergine
flour = use plain all purpose
        unless otherwise
        specified
pepitas = dried, untoasted
        pumpkin seeds
snow pea = mangetout
zucchini = courgettes
whitloof = Belgian endive or
        chicory

213 Miller Street, North Sydney, NSW 2060

Murdoch Books Food Editor: Jo Anne Calabria
Art Direction and Design: Elaine Rushbrooke
Photography: Ray Joyce
Illustrations: Barbara Rodanska
Editor: Lynn Humphries
Finished Art: Ivy Hansen
Index: Michael Wyatt

Publisher: Anne Wilson
Publishing Manager: Mark Newman
Managing Editor: Sarah Murray
Production Manager: Catie Ziller
Marketing Manager: Mark Smith

National Library of Australia
Cataloguing-in-Publication Data
Rosemary Stanton
Friendly Food
Includes index.
ISBN 0 86411 201 7
I. Recipes. I. Joyce, Ray
II. Title
641.563
First published 1992
Printed by Toppan Printing Co. Ltd, Singapore
Type by Adtype Graphics, North Sydney

Murdoch Books is a trademark of Murdoch Magazines Pty Ltd

Distributed in the UK, by Australian Consolidated Press (UK) Ltd,
20 Galowhill Road, Brackmills, Northhampton NN4 OEE
Enquiries — 0604 760456

The publisher thanks:
Accoutrement
Country Trader
Crafts Council, Sydney
Fragrant Garden
Immaterial Fabrics
Seasons Gallery
Waterford Wedgwood
Whitehill Silver and Plate Company
Wilsons Fabrics

Front Cover: Chilled Tomato Soup (page 23), Carpaccio of Salmon (page 26).
Back Cover: Chicken with Prunes and Nuts (page 57).

Frontispiece: Crunchy Mushroom Salad (page 74), Herbed Chicken (page 60) and Cucumber Salad (page 28),
Cornbread (page 36)